STITCH
SOMETHING
SPECIAL

A Farm Journal Craft Book

STITCH SOMETHING SPECIAL

More than 40 things to make from scraps

By Jean Gillies

FARM JOURNAL, INC.
Philadelphia, Pennsylvania

Distributed to the trade by
Doubleday & Company, Inc.
Garden City, New York

OTHER FARM JOURNAL CRAFT BOOKS

Let's Make a Patchwork Quilt

Let's Make More Patchwork Quilts

Soft Toys to Stitch and Stuff

Patterns for Appliqué and Pieced Work

Knit Sweaters the Easy Way

Scrap Saver's Stitchery Book

More Scrap Saver's Stitchery

Farm Journal's Homespun Christmas

Farm Journal's Design-and-Sew Children's Clothes

Easy Sewing with Knits

Modern Patchwork

Book Design: Michael P. Durning
Photography: Fred Carbone Studio
Illustrations: Len Epstein
Wall hangings, page 119,
   stitched by Jessie MacDonald

Library of Congress Cataloging in Publication Data
Gillies, Jean.
   Stitch something special.
   (A Farm journal craft book)
   Includes index.
   1. Sewing. 2. Textile fabrics. I. Title.
II. Series.
TT715.G55 1985 746.4 85-47685
ISBN 0-385-23173-3

CONTENTS

Sewing Guides

Through practice, everyone develops favorite sewing techniques. If you are an experienced seamstress or quilter, go ahead and use your own methods. If not, you can refer to the general guides in this chapter.

There are suggestions for preparing fabric; a list of helpful tools and supplies; and directions for tracing patterns, making templates, cutting fabric, stitching seams, appliquéing and quilting. There also are illustrations and directions for hand and embroidery stitches used in this book.

Preparing Fabric

If you're going to make something that will be washed, don't cut the fabric until you test it for colorfastness and preshrink it. (Even if the bolt is labeled "preshrunk," the fabric could shrink a little more.) This ensures that your finished work can be washed with no problems—and you won't be afraid to sponge away an accidental spot while you're working.

Preshrinking

Place each fabric piece in a pan of hot water, and leave it until the water is cool. If the water remains clear, put the fabric in the dryer or hang it up to dry.

If the color bleeds (runs), it may be a warning that the fabric will continue to bleed and ruin your finished project. But don't give up immediately—the problem may be excessive dye that will wash out. Change the water several times, then wash the fabric with detergent. After the fabric is dry, test it in water again. If the color still bleeds, eliminate that fabric.

The hot-water bath will preshrink the fabric. However, you may want to wash and dry the fabric, following the same laundry methods you plan to use for the finished item.

Removing creases

Before cutting fabric, remove all wrinkles and creases. Pressing with a steam iron may be all that's needed.

For a stubborn crease, place a damp cloth (wrung out) over the fabric and press with a dry iron. Lift and press along the crease. Remove cloth and press the fabric.

If any crease cannot be removed, try to place patterns so that the crease can be avoided when cutting fabric.

Tools and Supplies

Tracing paper: A roll of tracing paper is handy because you can cut off the size you need. If you use a pad, you can tape together several sheets to make a bigger sheet.

Oak tag board or similar weight material, such as a file folder, for making templates: It should be firm enough to keep its shape as you trace around it, yet thin enough to give fabric a sharp edge when you press an appliqué over it.

Shears: Try to keep one pair for cutting fabrics and another pair for paper. It's also helpful to have a good pair of embroidery scissors with points that cut right to the tips—to slash close to stitching and into points.

Compass for drawing circles, *ruler, carbon paper* for tracing patterns onto oak tag board, a *soft pencil* for marking light fabrics, and a *white dressmaker's pencil* for marking dark fabrics.

Open-toe presser foot for machine stitching over pencil lines. (It's difficult to see lines on the fabric when you have a presser foot that is closed in front.)

Plus: It's nice to have a *dressmaker's square* or *T-square* for making square corners and marking quilt blocks.

Tracing Patterns

To copy a pattern in this book, place tracing paper over pattern. Copy complete design, adding all special marks for assembling.

Copying a pattern in sections

In some cases, patterns are too large to fit on one page. These patterns are divided into sections with broken lines.

To trace, take a piece of tracing paper large enough for the full pattern. Trace each section, joining the sections on the broken lines.

Copying half a pattern

Sometimes only half a pattern is given. To trace, take a piece of paper large enough for the full pattern.

Fold paper in half. Open paper and place fold over broken fold line on pattern.

Trace the half pattern. Remove paper, refold, and copy pattern onto other half of paper. Cut out full pattern.

Making Templates

For tracing patterns on fabric, sometimes templates are used. These are pattern shapes cut from a firm material that keeps a good edge.

Simple template

To make a simple template, first use tracing paper to trace complete pattern from book.

Place tracing paper pattern over oak tag board or similar material. Slip a sheet of carbon paper between layers, and retrace pattern outline to copy it on the board. Cut out pattern shape.

(After using template to trace pattern shape on fabric, you can use the original paper pattern for marking inside design lines.)

Divided template

For an appliqué design that is divided into several sections (such as the dog in the Playtime Quilt), first make a template for the whole design, as for a simple template. Besides the outside shape, also copy inside lines that divide the shape into sections (the dog has three sections—body, face, ears).

Cut out the whole template. Then cut the template apart to make a separate template for each section.

(After using templates to trace pattern shapes, you can use the original paper pattern for marking inside design lines.)

Using Patterns on Fabric

A large pattern may be pinned to the fabric for cutting. For most patterns in this book, however, the pattern (tracing paper or template) is traced. Then the fabric is cut, either on the pencil line or with an added seam allowance.

Patterns for appliqués usually are traced, face up, on the right side of the fabric. Patterns for most other work are placed on the wrong side.

For tracing patterns, use a sharp soft pencil on light color fabrics and a white dressmaker's pencil on dark colors.

To mark batting, you can trace a pattern or template on some types. If you have trouble marking lines, place the pattern, template or fabric piece on the batting. Then cut around the shape.

Copying marks and design lines

After tracing or cutting around a pattern, mark fabric with any dots or lines that will be needed to match pattern pieces and assemble the item.

If inside design lines (for embroidery, topstitching, quilting, or positioning another fabric piece) must be added, you can use the paper pattern. Position pattern on right side of fabric. With a sharp soft pencil, punch holes through the pattern and make light dots along the needed lines. Remove pattern and connect dots with light pencil lines.

On dark fabric, first puncture paper with a sharp pencil, then mark fabric with a white dressmaker's pencil.

Note: If fabric is light, you may be able to trace lines through the fabric. To do this, first go over lines on pattern in ink. Then place pattern under fabric and mark fabric with light pencil lines.

Machine Stitching

Use matching thread for machine stitching unless directions call for a contrasting color.

Stay-stitching is done on a single layer of fabric after the fabric is cut. It is used at V points and inside curves to keep fabric from stretching and fraying when the seam allowance is slashed. It also is used to mark and secure seam edges that will be closed later with hand stitches.

To stay-stitch, use matching thread and a regular machine stitch. Follow the seam line or stitch just outside the seam line (in the seam allowance).

To machine-baste, lengthen the stitch and loosen the tension. Do not backstitch or tie thread ends; leave ends free. If the basting does not show when the item is finished, you can leave the basting in place. If basting should be removed, try to pull the bobbin thread. Clip threads at intervals to make shorter lengths.

To machine-gather, lengthen the stitch and loosen the tension, as for machine basting. Do not backstitch or tie thread ends; leave ends free. For long seams, break the stitching in half or in quarters, leaving threads at all seam ends free (do not stitch over cut threads).

To gather, pull bobbin thread at each end of the stitching and distribute the fullness evenly. To secure, pull threads to the back, tie pairs of threads into knots, and clip ends.

To stitch layers at a point (such as a sunray), stitch up one side to the point, take one stitch across the point, then stitch down the other side. This allows more room for the seam allowance to fit into the point area after fabric is turned to the right side.

Securing machine stitching is necessary at ends of seams. If a seam end will be crossed by another line of stitching, that is enough to hold it. For other seams, you can backstitch for a few stitches. You also can tie thread ends in a knot and clip the ends.

To secure thread ends on top-stitching (where backstitching or thread ends are not desirable), try this: Pull both thread ends to the surface and tie a small knot close to the fabric. Put the thread ends through a needle and take a long stitch between layers (do not catch the lower layer), bringing the needle up along the stitched line. Gently tug the thread and clip it close to the fabric. (When relaxed, thread ends will be hidden.)

Trimming Seams

After stitching, trim seams to reduce bulk. Clip off seam ends at an angle. At a point, cut off tip of point, and trim seam allowances on each side to $1/8''$.

At V points and inside curves, slash seam allowances to the stitching, being careful not to cut the stitching. This allows fabric to spread and lie flat when the seam allowance is turned under, or stitched layers are turned to the right side.

Pressing

After a seam is stitched, open the seam allowances and press them flat with an iron. A curved or shaped seam can be opened by running the tip of the iron along one seam allowance. After stitching two layers that will have an edge seam, turn fabric to the right side, work seam to the edge and press lightly.

In most cases, you should press seams with an iron, either a steam iron or a dry iron over a damp cloth. (Protect delicate fabrics by using a dry cloth under the damp one.)

There may be a few times when finger-pressing will be enough. Simply run your finger or fingernail along the seam to flatten it.

Stuffing

Polyester fiberfill is used to stuff the pillows and ornaments. Pull small wads of fiberfill from the bag and work them through the seam opening, keeping the surface smooth.

You can stuff large pillows by hand. For long, narrow areas (such as the Curly Snake), use a wooden spoon handle or other long tool. For small areas, use the smooth end of a crochet hook.

To stuff lightly, push the fiberfill gently into place and avoid creating lumps. To stuff firmly, use your hand or the tools to pack the fiberfill evenly.

Appliqué

For appliqué designs, use closely woven fabrics that won't fray easily. Otherwise, your work may pull apart.

Preparing appliqués

Most seam allowances on appliqués are turned to the wrong side. However, if a seam is covered by another appliqué, the bottom seam is left flat.

If a seam allowance is to be turned, stay-stitch any V points and inside curves. Then slash seam allowance to the stitching (Fig. 1). On outside curves, you can cut out small V-shaped pieces to reduce bulk.

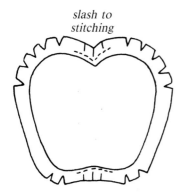

slash to stitching

Fig. 1 *Preparing appliqué*

Trim seam allowance to under ¼″ (or to ⅛″ in a narrow place) and turn to the wrong side. (For small curved pieces, it may help to place template on the wrong side and press the seam allowance over it.) Roll any stay-stitching to the wrong side so it won't show. Baste edges and press.

Lining an appliqué

When a solid color appliqué overlaps a print, or a light color overlaps a darker color, the bottom fabric may show through. To prevent this, underline the appliqué. Use a lightweight fabric in white or matching color.

Cut the lining the same shape, but omit the seam allowance. Place lining on the back of the appliqué before turning the seam allowance.

Attaching appliqués

Some appliqué designs are centered on the background fabric. To help find the center of the background, fold fabric in half crosswise and then lengthwise; press folds at center lightly with fingers.

To correctly place an appliqué, you can mark the appliqué outline on the background fabric with light pencil lines. One way is to position the template on top of the fabric and trace the outside shape. If the background fabric is light, another way is to place the paper pattern under the fabric for tracing. (First go over the pattern lines with ink to make them darker. Then mark fabric with light pencil lines.)

Position appliqué on background, pin in place and baste. Use matching thread and sew with an invisible hemming stitch (see page 5). If any pieces overlap, begin sewing on the bottom layer and end with the top layer.

Quilting

Quilting is done on three layers—a top and bottom layer of fabric and a middle layer of batting or fiberfill. Pin the layers together. To keep large areas from shifting, baste them together, sewing from the center to the outside edges.

To quilt by hand, use short quilting needles (also called Betweens). Quilting thread is best for large projects, but regular thread is fine for sewing a few short lines.

For most quilting in this book, you can hold the layers in your hands. For the large Playtime Quilt, you should use a quilting hoop or frame to keep the layers from shifting.

The quilting stitch is a short, even running stitch (see page 5), catching all layers with each stitch.

To hide a knot at the beginning of a new length of thread, bury it in the batting: Take a stitch through the quilt layers (from back to front), and gently tug the thread until the knot slips through the backing fabric into the batting.

To hide the thread end after stitching, make a knot in the thread, close to the fabric. Take one more stitch, pulling the knot through the top layer and into the batting (do not catch lower layer); bring the needle up along the stitching line, gently tug the thread, and clip the thread close to the fabric. *Note:* You can use the same methods for hiding knots and thread ends when you embroider a stuffed toy.

To quilt small projects by machine, use regular thread and a medium-to-long straight stitch. Test the stitch on fabric scraps the same thickness as the finished work.

Hand Stitches

Use matching thread for permanent stitches. For basting, use white or matching thread.

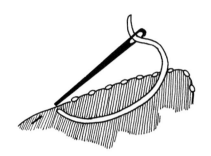

Hemming stitch for appliqué

Use thread to match the appliqué fabric. Bring needle up from wrong side of fabric, catching folded edge of appliqué. Take a diagonal stitch, inserting needle in background fabric close to where thread emerged; bring needle out ⅛″ ahead, through folded edge of appliqué.

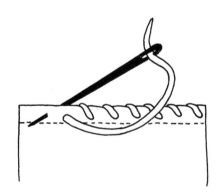

Overcast stitch

Use this to finish the raw edge of one or more layers of fabric to prevent raveling. With matching thread, take slanting stitches over the edge.

Running stitch

Work from right to left, making even stitches. Use small stitches for quilting and joining felt layers. Use longer stitches for basting.

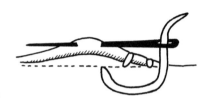

Slip stitch

This is an invisible stitch used to close a seam from the right side. Fold under the seam allowance on one side of the seam. Arrange fabric so that the folded edge overlaps seam allowance on other side of the seam.

Bring needle up through bottom layer on seam line. Take a small stitch through fold on top layer. Then take a stitch along seam line on bottom layer. Continue, alternating stitches through top fold and bottom layer. The finished seam should look as though it had been stitched from the wrong side.

Note: If the item to be stitched is flat, you will be joining two folded edges. Take a stitch through one fold, then the other, alternating stitches between the two folds.

Embroidery Stitches

Use two strands of floss for stitches. If you want a thicker line, use more strands.

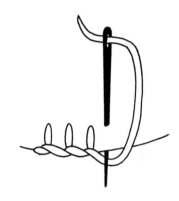

Blanket stitch

Use this to trim appliqué edges and to join felt layers. Work from left to right. Bring thread up from wrong side on embroidery line (or to edge of fabric). Hold thread with thumb and take a vertical stitch; bring needle out on embroidery line (or under edge of fabric) and over thread. Keep stitches uniform in depth and evenly spaced.

For trimming the edge of an appliqué, blanket stitches can be ³⁄₁₆″ deep and ⅛″ apart. For joining seams on small felt ornaments, the stitches can be less than ⅛″ deep and less than ⅛″ apart.

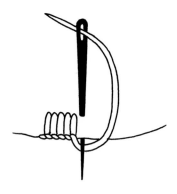

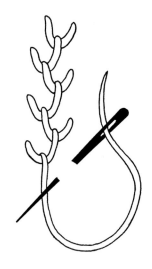

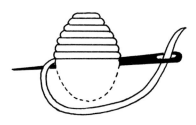

Buttonhole stitch

Work from left to right. Bring thread up from wrong side on embroidery line (or to edge of fabric). Hold thread with thumb and take a vertical stitch; bring needle out on embroidery line (or under edge of fabric) and over thread. Keep stitches close together with no space in between.

Feather stitch

Bring needle up through fabric on line to be stitched. Hold thread down with thumb and take a small slanted stitch slightly below and to the right; bring needle out at line and over thread. Take the next stitch slightly below and to the left of the line. Alternate stitches from right to left.

Satin stitch

Bring needle up on left side of design. Take a horizontal stitch, inserting needle on right side of design. Carry thread behind work, bringing needle up just under first stitch at left. Keep stitches parallel across the design and close together.

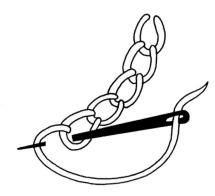

Stem stitch

Work from left to right. Take small backstitches, with each stitch overlapping the previous stitch. You can keep thread above or below needle, but be consistent.

Chain stitch

Work from right to left. Bring needle up from wrong side, and hold thread against fabric with thumb. Insert needle close to where thread came out and take a small stitch, bringing needle out over thread to form a loop. Continue, beginning the next stitch inside the loop to form a chain.

Tuck-in Gifts

A few scraps of fabric and a little of your time is all it takes to turn out one of these small items. They're fun things to tuck in with other gifts, especially those more practical, serious presents.

For example, a Plant Pal gives a lift to a common ivy or philodendron. A set of Kitchen Magnets adds appeal to a jar of homemade jelly or a set of measuring cups.

Tuck in a Baby's Doll with a box of disposable diapers. Gift-wrap a Baby's Soft Ball with a few knit shirts. Let a felt Scatter Pin add a whimsical touch to a Christmas sweater or a silk birthday scarf.

Of course, any one of these tuck-in gifts can be wrapped and given as a little remembrance or thank-you—all by itself.

PLANT PALS

From left to right: Flower Face, Big Bug and Green Worm (color photo, page 14)

Use one of these 5"-wide felt designs to brighten a leafy green plant, and you have a gift guaranteed to make someone smile. Seams are done in a blanket stitch, but you could use a running stitch for a faster finish.

Sew one end of wire to the felt layers, leaving the other end free to bury in the plant soil. Use 18-gauge wire that's painted green—it's sold with flower-making craft supplies.

Green Worm

Head and body are cut separately. Of course, real worms don't have antennae, but this felt worm has big yellow ones.

MATERIALS
Green felt, 6x8"
Yellow felt, 2½x5"
Embroidery floss in black and
  colors to match felt
Polyester fiberfill
12" of 18-gauge wire

DIRECTIONS

Join felt layers with matching floss and a blanket stitch. Use two strands of floss for all stitching.

For extra help with patterns, templates and stitching, see *Sewing Guides,* page 1.

Cut patterns and felt

1. Trace pattern pieces for Green Worm, page 16, and make templates. Seam allowances are included.

2. Place templates on two layers of felt. On yellow, trace antennae. On green, trace body. Cut out on pencil lines.

3. On two layers of green felt, trace head. Use paper pattern to copy lines for face.

Before cutting, embroider face on top layer. Use yellow floss, with a stem stitch for mouth and a satin stitch for eyes. With black floss, take two satin stitches in the center of each eye.

Place embroidered felt over bottom layer and cut out head on pencil line.

Assemble worm

4. Pin body layers together and stitch edges with green floss. Stuff lightly as you close each curve; leave curve at head end open between dots.

5. Insert wire between body layers; work it through stitches at bottom edge and bring to the top opening. At top end of wire, bend ½" into a loop.

Sew loop to body, keeping loop above line where head will be attached.

6. Pin head layers together and stitch from dot to dot; leave bottom open. Stuff lightly and position head over body and wire. Attach front and back of head to body.

7. Stitch antennae layers together with yellow floss; add a little fiberfill before closing.

Position antennae on back of head and attach with hidden stitches.

Flower Face

Make five petals and stitch them to the flower center. Try a variety of color combinations.

MATERIALS

Bright pink felt, 9x12"
White felt, 2½" square
Embroidery floss in blue and colors to match felt
Polyester fiberfill
12" of 18-gauge wire

DIRECTIONS

Join felt layers with matching floss and a blanket stitch. Use two strands of floss for all stitching.

For extra help with patterns, templates and stitching, see *Sewing Guides,* page 1.

Cut patterns and felt

1. Trace pattern pieces for Flower Face, page 16, and make templates. Seam allowances are included.

2. On two layers of pink felt, trace five petals. On single layer of pink felt, trace one flower center. Cut out on pencil lines.

3. On single layer of white felt, trace one flower center. Use paper pattern to copy lines for face.

Before cutting, embroider face. Use pink floss and a stem stitch for mouth. Use blue floss and a satin stitch for eyes, ending in one straight stitch for the nose.

Cut out on pencil line.

Assemble flower

4. For each petal, pin layers together and stitch outside curve with pink floss; leave straight edge open.

Stuff each petal lightly and take a small tuck (¼") in center of straight edge.

5. Arrange petals to form a circle, with each petal overlapping an adjacent petal (Fig. 1). Sew together at center to hold.

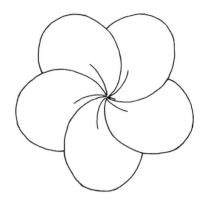

Fig. 1 *Arranging petals*

6. At one end of wire, bend ½" into a loop. Place loop against center back of petals and sew in place.

7. Place pink flower center over wire and pin in place. Attach with pink floss; tuck in a little fiberfill before closing.

8. Center embroidered face on front and pin in place. Attach with white floss; tuck in a little fiberfill before closing.

Big Bug

Combine three felt colors to make this fat bug with a big smile.

MATERIALS

Yellow felt, 8x9"
Orange felt, 3x5½"
Teal felt, 5½" square
Embroidery floss in black and colors to match felt
Polyester fiberfill
12" of 18-gauge wire

DIRECTIONS

Join felt layers with matching floss and a blanket stitch. Use two strands of floss for all stitching.

For extra help with patterns, templates and stitching, see *Sewing Guides,* page 1.

Cut patterns and felt

1. Trace pattern pieces for Big Bug, page 17, and make templates. Seam allowances are included.

2. On two layers of yellow felt, trace antennae. On single layer of yellow felt, trace wing back and wing front, top section. On single layer of orange, trace wing front, bottom section. Cut out on pencil lines.

3. On two layers of teal felt, trace body. Use paper pattern to copy lines for face.

Before cutting, embroider face on top layer. Use yellow floss, with a stem stitch for mouth and a satin stitch for eyes. With black floss, take two satin stitches in the center of each eye.

Place embroidered felt over bottom layer and cut out body on pencil line.

Assemble bug

4. Pin wing front, top section (yellow) over wing front, bottom section (orange) and pin. (To check position, lay both pieces over back piece.) Stitch with yellow floss.

5. Pin wing front unit to wing back. Stitch together, using floss to match front sections; stuff lightly with fiberfill before closing.

6. At one end of wire, bend ½″ into a loop. Center loop on back of wings and sew in place.

7. Pin body layers together. Stitch around head from dot to dot with matching floss. Stuff head lightly.

Position front layer of body over front of wings, and back layer of body over back of wings. Sew back layer in place, with wire running down the center to tip of body; stuff lightly before closing.

Stitch front of body to wings and to back of body below wings; stuff lightly before closing.

8. Pin antennae layers together. Join with yellow floss, adding a little fiberfill before closing.

Position antennae on back of head and attach with hidden stitches.

KITCHEN MAGNETS

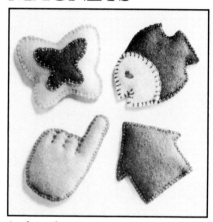

(color photo, page 11)

Choose one of these four hand-stitched designs, and make a set of three to tuck in with a gift of food or a kitchen utensil. There's an Arrow, Butterfly, Fish and Pointed Finger.

The designs are easy to make. They look fancy when you join the felt pieces with blanket stitches, but you could substitute short running stitches to finish them even faster.

For the magnet, use a flexible magnetic strip which can be cut into smaller pieces. This has an adhesive backing and is sold with craft supplies.

MATERIALS
Felt scraps
Embroidery floss in matching and contrasting colors
Polyester fiberfill
1″ lengths of magnetic strip, ¾″ wide

DIRECTIONS
Use two strands of floss for all stitching. For extra help with patterns, templates and hand stitches, see *Sewing Guides,* page 1.

Cut patterns and felt

1. Trace pattern pieces, page 18, and make templates. Seam allowances are included.

2. Trace templates on felt and cut out.

For Arrow, use double layer of one color and trace template.

For Butterfly, use two colors. On double layer of one color, trace butterfly. On single layer of second color, trace one trim.

For Fish, use two colors. On single layer of one color, trace one body and one tail section. On single layer of second color, trace one face.

For Pointed Finger, use double layer of one color and trace template. For fingernail trim (optional), trace nail template on single layer of second color.

Assemble design

3. For two-color designs only, assemble top layer. Arrange felt pieces and sew together, using matching or contrasting floss and a blanket stitch.

For Butterfly, center trim on top layer and stitch in place.

For Fish, let face overlap tail section and stitch in place. (To check position, lay both sections over body piece.)

For Pointed Finger, position nail on finger and stitch in place.

4. If design has embroidery (Fish; optional on Arrow), use paper pattern to mark lines on top layer. Embroider with contrasting floss.

For Fish, use a satin stitch for eye.

For Arrow, use a stem stitch for mouth and a group of straight stitches crossed at center for eyes.

5. Pin and stitch felt layers together. Use matching or contrasting floss and a blanket stitch; stuff lightly with fiberfill before closing.

For Pointed Finger, first use a running stitch to sew lines between fingers. Then go around the outside edge with a blanket stitch.

6. Press piece of magnetic strip to back of design.

SCATTER PINS

Some of the small patterns used for other projects in this book can be made into soft jewelry to wear on a scarf, sweater or coat lapel. Most designs need only a pin added to the back, and you can buy special pin backs at craft supply shops. In a few cases, you will need to stitch an extra piece of fabric to the back before adding the pin.

For an Arrow, Butterfly, Fish or Pointed Finger, follow directions under *Kitchen Magnets,* page 9. To finish, omit the magnetic strip and add a pin back.

For a Spider, use felt and chenille stems in colors to match or contrast. Follow directions under *Spider Web Shoulder Bag,* page 62 (see Steps 12-14). Add a pin back.

For a Ruffled Flower, use any color fabric. Follow directions under *Ruffled Flower Fabric Picture,* page 95 (see Steps 3-4). To finish back, mark a 2¼" circle on matching fabric. Cut out, adding a ⅛" seam allowance. Turn seam allowance to wrong side, baste and press. Hand-stitch circle to back of flower, and add a pin back.

For a Sun Face, use yellow or orange fabric with contrasting floss for embroidery. Follow directions under *Sun Face Belt Purse,* page 51 (see Step 8). Add a pin back.

FELT PICTURES

You can create a little picture for the wall, like the Fish picture shown on page 85. Make the Fish or the Butterfly under *Kitchen Magnets,* page 9. Omit the magnetic strip.

Use a small frame (small ones are sold in needlework shops for framing cross-stitch work).

Cut a piece of felt for the background, about 1" larger than frame opening. Attach Fish or Butterfly to center of felt with a few hidden stitches.

Fold edges of felt background over frame backing (inner piece of fiberboard or cardboard) and secure with masking tape or white glue.

Place felt picture in frame and secure to frame edges.

BABY'S DOLL

(color photo, page 83)

Small and soft and easy to make, this could be Baby's first doll. Only 7½" tall, it's simply a fabric body with a heart-shaped felt face and a few yarn curls. You can use a checked gingham fabric like the one shown, or a small print. Just be sure all materials are washable.

The felt face is attached with embroidery floss and a blanket stitch. To save time, you could use regular white thread and a small running stitch.

MATERIALS
Small-check gingham or a print fabric, 9x14", for body
White felt scrap, for face
5" yellow yarn, for curls
White and yellow thread
Embroidery floss in black, red and color to match fabric
Polyester fiberfill

DIRECTIONS
For extra help with patterns, stitching and stuffing, see *Sewing Guides,* page 1.

(continued on page 15)

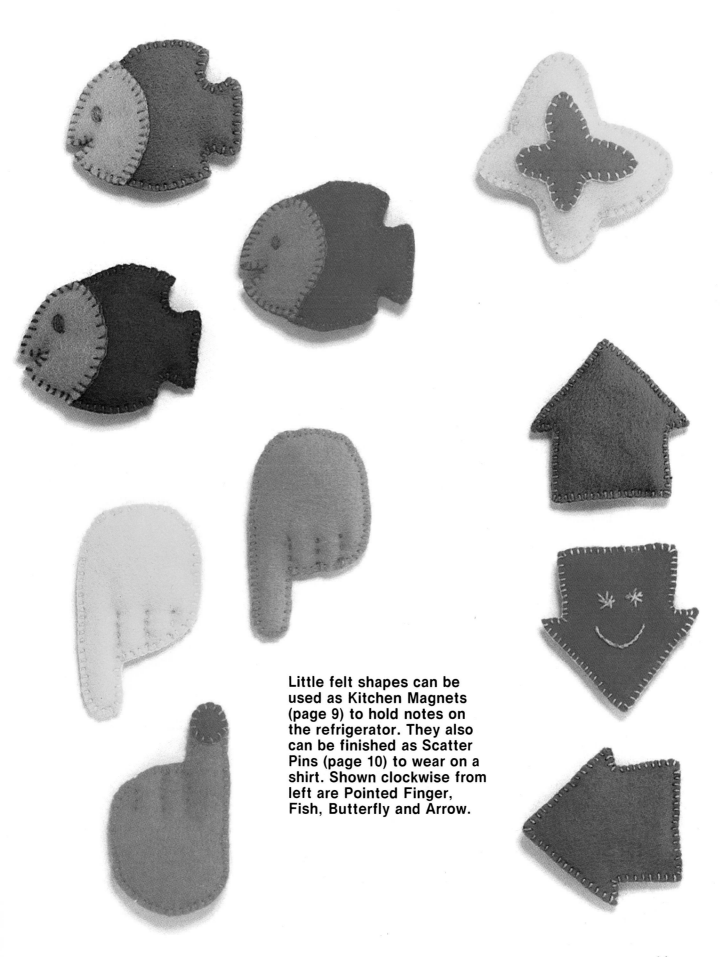

Little felt shapes can be used as Kitchen Magnets (page 9) to hold notes on the refrigerator. They also can be finished as Scatter Pins (page 10) to wear on a shirt. Shown clockwise from left are Pointed Finger, Fish, Butterfly and Arrow.

Stuffed toys will please children of all ages. Choose Floppy Clown with green and black felt eyes (page 22), Curly Snake with a wide red mouth (page 21) or Red Monster with big white teeth (page 24).

Felt Plant Pals (page 7) add a bit of color to a green plant. Left to right are Flower Face, Green Worm and Big Bug—all with happy smiles to embroider.

(continued from page 10)

Cut patterns and fabric

1. Trace patterns for body and face, page 19, and cut out. Seam allowances for body will be added when cutting fabric.

2. Fold fabric for body in half, with right side inside. (Gingham is the same on both sides.) Pin body pattern on top and trace. Mark dots for face position and for opening. Cut out body, adding ¼″ seam allowance.

3. On white felt, trace doll face and mark features. Cut out on pencil outline.

Assemble doll

4. Take each body layer, and machine-stitch along seam line between dots for opening (¼″ from edge). This keeps the fabric from stretching or fraying and will be a guide when you close the doll after stuffing.

5. Work with top layer of body. On right side, position felt face. (Push pins through fabric from wrong side to locate top and bottom dots for face.) Baste face in place, ¼″ from edge of felt.

6. Embroider face with two strands of floss and a chain stitch. Use black floss for eyes and red for mouth.

7. Attach face with a blanket stitch, using two strands of floss to match fabric.

8. Pin body pieces, right sides together. Stitch on pencil line, leaving bottom open for turning. Clip inside curves at neck and arms and turn to right side.

9. Stuff each arm lightly and pin fabric flat. With a double strand of white thread, make a row of small running stitches to define arm (Fig. 2).

10. Stuff doll lightly, keeping head and body somewhat flat. Close opening with slip stitches.

11. To add hair trim, first thread needle with yellow thread and knot one end.

Wrap the 5″ of yellow yarn around a pencil. With threaded needle, sew through yarn, catching both cut ends. Slide yarn off pencil and secure loops with more stitches; do not cut thread. Sew curls above face.

Fig. 2 *Stitching arms*

BABY'S SOFT BALLS

(color photo, page 83)

You can roll or toss these balls without hurting Baby because they're stuffed with fiberfill. (They'll even take a small bounce.)

Each ball is made from two pieces of fabric, stitched together in one continuous seam. The small size measures about 9½″ in circumference, and the large one measures about 12½″.

Choose a washable, medium-weight knit fabric with some stretch, such as a stretch flannel or a doubleknit. Avoid a fabric that is too thin—it will be difficult to shape and may end up with a lumpy look.

For trim, work a feather stitch over the seam.

MATERIALS

Knit fabric, 8x10½″ (with stretch along the 10½″ measure), for large ball *or* 7x9″ (with stretch along the 9″ measure), for small ball
Thread to match fabric
Embroidery floss in contrasting color
Polyester fiberfill

DIRECTIONS

For extra help with patterns, stitching and stuffing, see *Sewing Guides*, page 1.

Cut pattern and fabric

1. Trace pattern for one of the balls, page 20, and cut out. Seam allowances will be added when cutting fabric.

2. Pin pattern to wrong side of knit, with arrows running in direction of stretch. Trace pattern twice, leaving space for ¼″ seam allowances. Copy marks for ends and centers. On one piece, copy dots for opening. Do not cut fabric.

Assemble ball

3. By machine, stay-stitch fabric on pencil lines. Cut out the two pieces, adding ¼″ seam allowances. Clip seam allowances to stitching along inside curves.

4. Pin the two pieces, right sides together, matching the two end marks on each piece to the center marks on the other piece. Baste the seam.

Machine-stitch a continuous seam, leaving an opening for turning. Remove basting and turn to right side.

5. Stuff ball with fiberfill, shaping it as you work. Use enough fiberfill to make a firm round shape. Close opening with slip stitches.

6. For trim, use two or three strands of contrasting floss and work a feather stitch over the seam.

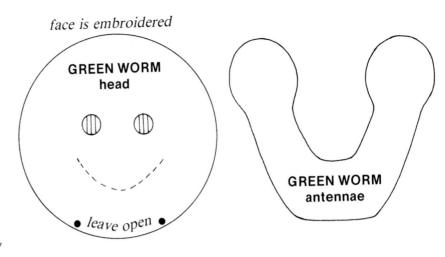

face is embroidered

GREEN WORM head

leave open

GREEN WORM antennae

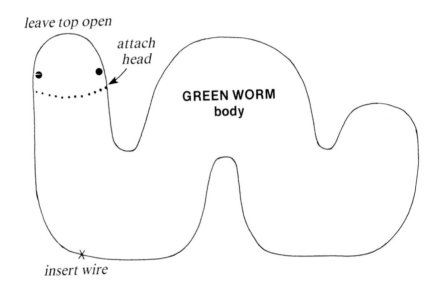

leave top open

attach head

GREEN WORM body

insert wire

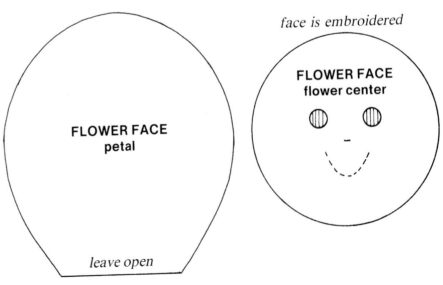

face is embroidered

FLOWER FACE petal

leave open

FLOWER FACE flower center

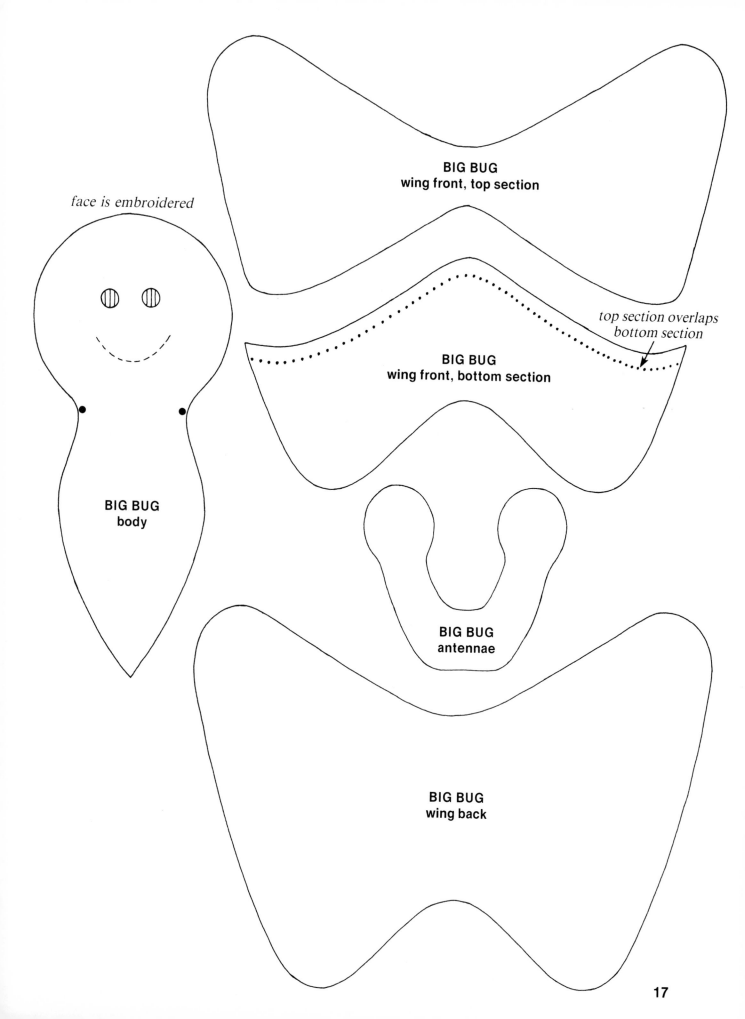

face is embroidered

BIG BUG
body

BIG BUG
wing front, top section

BIG BUG
wing front, bottom section

top section overlaps
bottom section

BIG BUG
antennae

BIG BUG
wing back

17

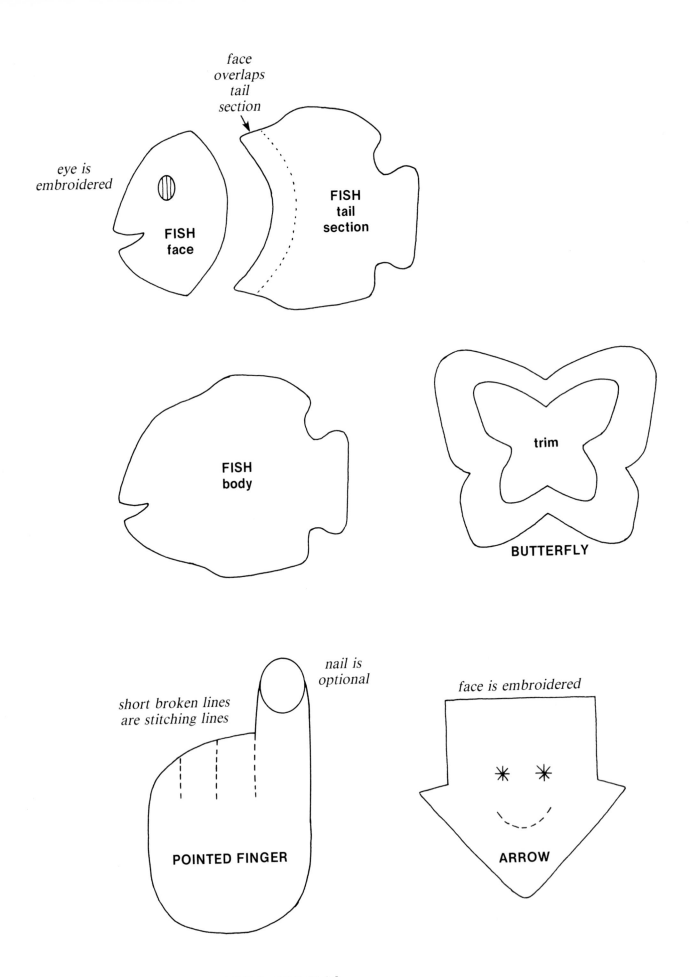

face
overlaps
tail
section

eye is
embroidered

**FISH
tail
section**

**FISH
face**

**FISH
body**

trim

BUTTERFLY

nail is
optional

short broken lines
are stitching lines

POINTED FINGER

face is embroidered

ARROW

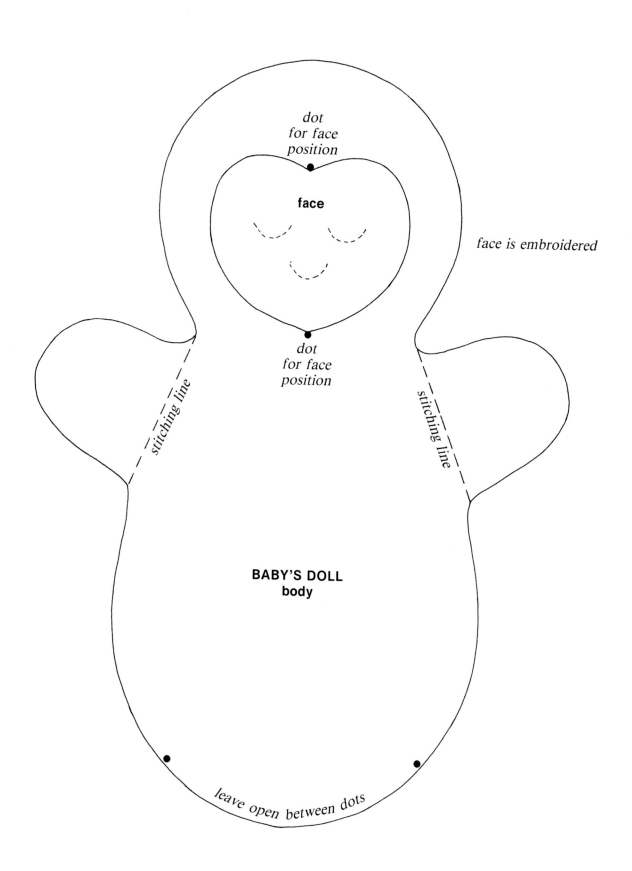

dot
for face
position

face

face is embroidered

stitching line

dot
for face
position

stitching line

BABY'S DOLL
body

leave open between dots

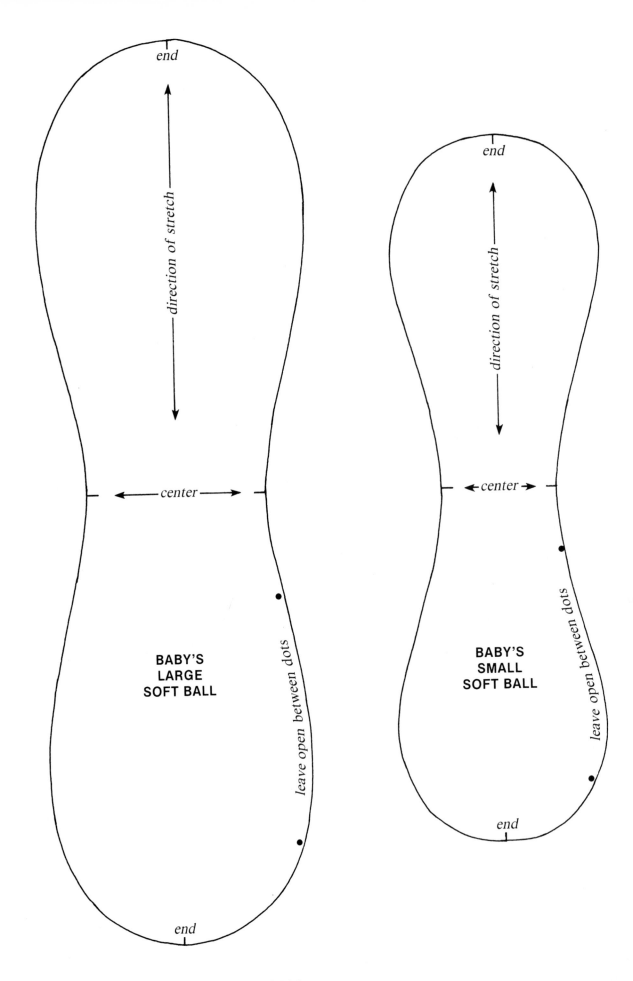

end

direction of stretch

← *center* →

**BABY'S
LARGE
SOFT BALL**

leave open between dots

end

end

direction of stretch

←*center*→

**BABY'S
SMALL
SOFT BALL**

leave open between dots

end

Stuffed Toys

Soft toys aren't just for little folks. There are children and adults of all ages who find pleasure in owning stuffed dolls and animals, like the Curly Snake, Floppy Clown or Red Monster in this chapter. You can make one for a child's play toy, and finish another one for an adult to use as a light-hearted decoration.

The clown looks interesting by himself, perched on a bookshelf with one leg dangling over the edge. For a pair of toys, stitch the clown and snake and arrange them together on a bed, bench or even the floor.

(If you want to make a small doll or ball for a baby, you'll find directions in the previous chapter on Tuck-in Gifts.)

CURLY SNAKE

(color photo, page 12)

This friendly snake has a spiral body, so it coils naturally. You can drape it over a chair, set it on a pile of pillows, or stack several together. Use felt for the eyes and add a jingle bell on a ribbon for trim.

MATERIALS
½ yd. print, 44″ wide, for body
Red fabric, 6″ square,
  for mouth
Red and black felt scraps,
  for eyes
Thread to match fabric and felt
Polyester fiberfill
½ yd. red ribbon, ¼″ wide
1 jingle bell, ⅝″ diameter

DIRECTIONS
Dressmaker's carbon paper is used for marking fabric. For extra help with patterns, templates, stitching and stuffing, see *Sewing Guides,* page 1.

Cut patterns and fabric
1. Trace full pattern for snake, pages 27-30, joining sections on broken lines. Cut out around shape. Trace half pattern for mouth, page 28; make full pattern and cut out. Also trace patterns for inner and outer eyes, page 27, and make templates. Seam allowances are included.

2. Fold print fabric in half, right side inside. Pin snake pattern on top and trace around outside. Slip dressmaker's carbon paper under pattern to mark spiral cutting line and seam openings. Remove pattern and carbon paper, and pin fabric together in a few places. Cut out fabric around head only, following marks indicated on pattern. (Body spiral will be stitched before cutting.)

Pin mouth pattern to wrong side of red fabric and trace. Use dressmaker's carbon to mark dart. Remove pattern and cut out fabric.

Assemble snake

3. On wrong side of mouth, fold, pin and stitch dart. Clip dart to stitching at widest point and press dart to one side. Fold mouth in half, right side inside (Fig. 1), and press. Then fold right side out (but don't press).

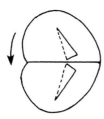

Fig. 1 *Folding mouth*

4. Pin mouth to each layer of snake body, right sides together, matching center points and dots A and B. For machine stitching, use red thread on top and thread to match body in bobbin. With mouth on top, stitch curve between dots A and B; take ¼″ seams. Turn snake over and stitch curve on other half of mouth.

5. To stitch body (Fig. 2), begin at dot A on outside edge of head (this continues line of stitching from mouth). Stitch ¼″ from cutting line, going to tip of tail, around tip, and back to dot B on opposite side of head; leave two openings, as indicated on pattern.

Carefully cut fabric along cutting line (between stitched lines). To mark seam lines at openings, stay-stitch the single layers ¼″ from cut edges.

Slash seam allowances along inside curve of body and neck, making cuts about ½″ apart. Use tip of iron to press seam open. Turn to right side through neck opening. Work seam to edge and finger-press.

Stuff and trim

6. Begin stuffing end of body through opening near tail. Use small amounts of fiberfill and push in place with a long blunt tool, such as a wooden spoon handle. Keep the stuffing smooth and uniform. From the same opening, stuff body in other direction, about halfway to neck opening.

From neck opening, finish stuffing body. Also stuff head, keeping mouth area somewhat flat.

7. Close openings with slip stitches, tucking in extra fiberfill as needed.

8. For eyes, trace templates and cut two outer eyes of red felt and two inner eyes of black felt. Sew outer eyes to head with red thread and small running stitches. Then add inner eyes with black thread.

9. Draw red ribbon through jingle bell and tie ribbon around snake's neck.

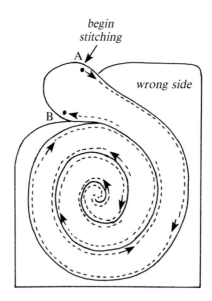

Fig. 2 *Stitching body*

FLOPPY CLOWN

(color photos, pages 12-13)

Drape one of these 22″-long characters on a shelf or against a lamp. The one-piece body (with head) is stuffed. Arms and legs, formed by the suit, are loose. The mitts and slippers attached to the suit have weights inside, so you can arrange the clown in a variety of poses.

Use a print fabric for the suit, and a solid color for the mitts and slippers. The cap can be of either fabric.

Eyes are felt. You can cut the nose and mouth from felt, too, or you can embroider them.

MATERIALS

⅔ yd. print, 44″ wide, for suit and cap
Solid color fabric, 9x14″, for mitts and slippers (plus 7x12″ piece for cap, if desired)
Firm white fabric, 13″ square, for body
Green and black felt scraps, for face (red felt for nose and mouth is optional)

Thread to match fabric and felt
Embroidery floss in black and
  white (plus red if mouth is
  embroidered)
White pompons, 1″ diameter:
  2 for suit trim, plus 2 for
  slippers (optional)
4 egg sinkers (weights, ½ oz.
  each, available at sporting
  goods stores)

DIRECTIONS

For extra help with patterns,
templates, stitching and stuffing, see *Sewing Guides,* page 1.

Cut patterns and fabric

1. Trace half pattern for
body, page 31; add 2″ to extend
body as indicated. Make full
pattern.

Trace half pattern for suit,
pages 32-33, joining sections on
broken lines; add 4″ to extend
at neck as indicated. Make full
pattern.

Trace pattern pieces for cap,
page 34, and for slipper and
mitt, page 31. Trace patterns
for eyelid and eye trim, page
34, and make templates. If nose
and mouth are to be of felt,
trace those patterns and make
templates.

Cut out full patterns and
templates. Seam allowances are
included.

2. Fold white fabric in half,
right side outside. Pin full body
pattern on top. Trace around
pattern and copy lines for face.
(If nose and mouth are to be of
felt, lines for those features will
be guides for placing the appliqués.) Cut out body on pencil
line.

Fold print fabric in half,
right side inside, with selvages
together. Pin suit pattern on
top and cut out; copy marks
for tucks at shoulders. If cap is
to be of print, trace front and
back pieces on single layer and
cut out.

Fold solid color fabric in
half, right side inside. On top,

trace two mitts and two slippers; on each slipper, mark the
inside curve. If cap is to be of
solid color, trace pieces on
single layer. Cut out on pencil
lines.

Use templates to trace two
eyelids on green felt and two
eye trims on black felt. Cut out
on pencil lines.

Make body

3. Complete face. Position
green eyelids on face and attach
with green thread, sewing over
the felt edges.

With two strands of black
floss and a chain stitch, embroider around eyelids and
along lower edges of eyes. Also
embroider eyebrows.

Position black eye trims and
attach with black thread, sewing over the felt edges. For eye
highlights, use white floss and
take three or four small satin
stitches on each black eye trim
(see pattern for placement).

*For embroidered mouth and
nose:* Use two strands of floss.
Work red mouth with a chain
stitch. Form black nose with
two straight stitches.

For felt mouth and nose: Use
templates to cut pieces from red
felt. Position on face and attach with red thread, sewing
over the felt edges.

4. To mark seam lines along
body opening, stay-stitch each
single layer between dots, ¼″
from edge of fabric.

5. Pin body pieces, right sides
together. Stitch a ¼″ seam,
leaving an opening on one side
for turning. Slash inside curves
at neck, and press seam open
with tip of iron. Trim corners.

To square off bottom, fold
fabric so the bottom seam is
centered and running against
one side seam to form a
triangle (Fig. 3). Measure 1″
from tip of triangle. Mark
and stitch across base of
triangle (a).

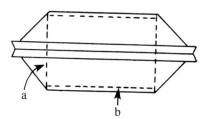

Fig. 3 *Squaring off body
along bottom seam*

Repeat to stitch triangle at
opposite end of seam. Then
fold fabric to connect ends of
the triangles to form a rectangle. Stitch along each fold,
just catching the fold (b). Turn
body to right side.

6. Stuff body firmly with
fiberfill, keeping head somewhat flat. Close opening with
slip stitches.

Make suit

7. Pin edges of suit, right
sides together. Stitch ¼″ seams,
leaving openings at neck and at
ends of sleeves and legs.

Clip inside curves. Open
seams and press flat; work on
edge of an ironing board or use
a rolled-up washcloth under
seams to avoid creasing fabric.
Turn suit to right side and press
seams again.

8. Turn neck edge 2¾″ to
wrong side, pin and press. Turn
edge of each sleeve and leg 1″
to wrong side, pin and press.

9. At each shoulder, take a
1¼″ tuck (Fig. 4) and secure
with a few hand stitches on the
seam line.

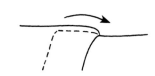

Fig. 4 *Making tuck*

Make mitts and slippers

10. On the top layer of each slipper, transfer curve to right side by basting along pencil line.

11. Pin the two layers of each slipper and mitt, right sides together, and stitch; leave straight edge open for turning. Turn to right side and press.

12. Tuck a little fiberfill into the tip of each slipper and mitt.

On each slipper, pin fabric layers flat and use machine to topstitch inside curve (Fig. 5). Add a little more fiberfill.

Fig. 5 *Topstitching slipper*

13. Cushion each egg sinker by wrapping it with fiberfill and then with thread. Insert a weight in each slipper and mitt, adding more fiberfill if needed.

Close each opening by hand with small running stitches, ½″ from straight edge; gather to measure 1″ across, and secure.

Assemble clown

14. To make ruffles on suit, begin working on the 1″ fold inside one leg. Use a double strand of thread and make a small running stitch by hand, ¼″ from the raw edge; catch folded layer to right side (Fig. 6). Pull thread to gather, but do not secure.

Insert slipper in leg and adjust ruffle to fit. By hand, attach gathered seam on slipper to gathered seam of ruffle.

Repeat steps to make ruffles on the other leg and on both sleeves. Attach a slipper to other leg, and attach a mitt to each sleeve.

15. Make the neck ruffle in the same way. Insert body in suit and pull thread to gather ruffle around neck. Attach ruffle to body.

16. To make cap, stay-stitch each piece along bottom curve, ¼″ from edge. Slash seam allowance to stitching along inside curve on cap front.

Pin cap pieces, right sides together, matching dots. Stitch a ¼″ seam around curve. Open seam with tip of iron and turn to right side. Turn raw edge of cap to wrong side, pin and press.

17. Tuck a little fiberfill inside the top curve of cap. Place cap on head, keeping it at least ¼″ from eyebrows. Attach bottom edge to head with slip stitches.

18. Trim suit front with two pompons. Add a pompon to each slipper, if you like.

19. For cap trim (optional), cut a red felt heart, using pattern on page 34. By hand, sew heart to one side of cap.

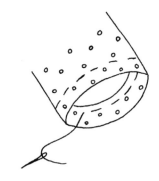

Fig. 6 *Gathering ruffle*

RED MONSTER

(color photo, page 13)

It has pointed teeth and horns, and if you make it in red, this creature looks like a dragon. The finished size is 13½″ tall and 18½″ long.

Choose a firm, medium-weight fabric that doesn't ravel. A slipcover fabric gives the monster a textured surface, but denim also would be a good choice. Use lightweight fabrics for the mouth, eyes and teeth.

MATERIALS
1 yd. red fabric, 44″ wide
Bright green fabric, 7x16″, for mouth and eyes
White fabric, 7½x10″, for teeth
Black felt scrap, for eye pupils and nostrils
Thread to match fabrics
Green and black embroidery floss
Polyester fiberfill

DIRECTIONS
Stitch ¼″ seams with thread to match fabric. For some seams, pieces are not cut the same length. In those cases, match dots at seam ends, and stitch from dot to dot; do not stitch into seam allowances. These seams are noted in the directions.

For extra help with patterns, templates, stitching and stuffing, see *Sewing Guides,* page 1.

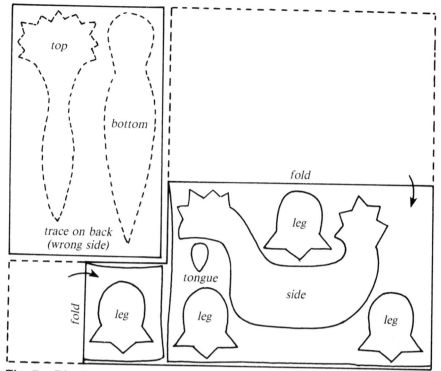

Fig. 7 *Placing pattern pieces on fabric*

Cut patterns and fabric

1. Trace pattern for side, pages 35-38, joining sections on broken lines. Trace half patterns for top, page 39, and bottom, page 40, joining sections on broken lines; make full patterns. Trace half pattern for mouth, page 38, and make full pattern.

Also trace patterns for eye, tongue and nostril, page 36, and for teeth and leg, page 41.

Cut out full patterns, and make templates for the eye, pupil and nostril. Seam allowances are included on all patterns except the eye.

2. Pin pattern pieces to wrong side of red fabric, with straight of grain line running along lengthwise grain (see Fig. 7).

On single layer, pin top and bottom pieces, and trace. Cut out on pencil lines.

Fold remaining fabric to make two layers, right side inside. On top, pin side piece and tongue and trace. Also trace leg pattern four times. Cut out on pencil lines.

Fold white and green fabrics to make a double layer of each, right sides inside. On white, trace one upper teeth and one lower teeth. On green, trace mouth. Cut out on pencil lines.

Open green fabric to make single layer. Place eye template on right side and trace twice. Cut out, adding ¼" seam allowances.

Stitch trims and stay-stitch

3. Stitch upper teeth layers, right sides together; leave straight edge open. Stitch lower teeth layers in the same way. Trim seams and slash into V points. Turn to right side and press lightly.

Stuff each teeth unit lightly with fiberfill. Pin raw edges together and machine-stitch ¼" from edge. Slash seam allowance almost to stitching at ½" intervals.

4. Pin mouth layers along straight edges, right sides together. Stitch from dot to dot only.

5. On large red pieces (side, top and bottom), stay-stitch seam lines along inside curves and at V points where indicated on patterns. Then slash seam allowances almost to the stitching. Also stay-stitch one side piece and the bottom piece along edges that will be left open for turning.

6. Pin and stitch neck dart on bottom piece. Press.

Assemble monster

7. Pin top piece to one side piece, matching horns; also match dots at A (head) and B (tail). Baste and stitch from dot to dot only.

Pin, baste and stitch top piece to other side piece.

Trim seams and slash into V points.

8. Pin short ends of side pieces together (in front of horns). Stitch from dot A to raw edges.

Turn fabric to right side, work each seam to edge and press horns lightly.

9. Using paper pattern for side, position horn section over fabric, letting seam allowances on pattern extend beyond fabric. Mark line for topstitching on fabric.

Stuff horns lightly. Pin fabric flat along pencil line, and topstitch line (Fig. 8).

Turn fabric over. Mark and topstitch line on other side.

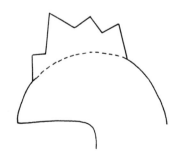

Fig. 8 *Topstitching below horns*

Fig. 9 *Basting teeth in place*

10. Center upper teeth on seam where side pieces are joined (in front of horns), right sides together. Pin and baste in place (Fig. 9).

Center lower teeth on bottom piece, right sides together, and baste in place.

11. Center one layer of mouth over upper teeth, right sides together; match dots at sides of mouth to C dots on side pieces. Baste and stitch from dot to dot only.

Center other layer of mouth over lower teeth, right sides together; match dots at sides of mouth to C dots on bottom piece. Baste and stitch from dot to dot.

12. Pin bottom piece to each side piece, right sides together; match C dots at mouth and D dots at tail. Stitch from dot to dot; leave opening on one seam (along stay-stitching) for turning.

13. To close tail, pin sides together between dots. Stitch from dot to dot.

14. Trim and slash seam allowances at V points and inside curves on all seams. Turn monster to right side and work seams to the edge.

Check corners of mouth. If there is a gap, close it from the right side with slip stitches.

Stuff and trim

15. Place side pattern over fabric at tail, letting seam allowance on pattern extend beyond fabric. Mark line for topstitching on fabric.

Stuff tail points lightly. Pin fabric layers flat along marked line, and topstitch curve.

16. Stuff monster firmly, shaping head and body as you work. On chin, turn lower teeth upward, pushing stuffing against seam allowance. Keep lower mouth somewhat flat.

From right side, push your hand into mouth opening to help shape head and mouth.

After stuffing, close opening on lower edge of monster with slip stitches.

17. To make legs, stitch each unit, right sides together; leave opening for turning.

Trim seam and slash into V points. Turn to right side and press lightly.

On each leg, place pattern over fabric and mark line for topstitching. Stuff toes lightly. Pin layers flat along stitching line and topstitch across each leg.

Stuff rest of each leg lightly and close opening with slip stitches.

18. Position legs on body and attach along top curve with hand stitches. Also catch inside layer of leg to body with a few hidden stitches, about ½" above topstitched line on leg.

19. Begin eyes by turning raw edge of each green circle to wrong side. Baste and press.

On black felt, trace two eye pupils and cut out on pencil lines.

Center a black felt circle on each green eye and attach with two strands of green floss and a blanket stitch.

20. Position eyes on monster and pin in place. Attach with a hemming stitch, tucking in a little fiberfill before closing. For trim, go around each eye again, using two strands of green floss and a blanket stitch.

21. For nose, trace two nostrils on black felt and cut out on pencil lines. Position above teeth and attach with black floss and a blanket stitch.

22. To make tongue, stitch the two layers, right sides together; leave opening for turning. Trim seam, turn to right side and press lightly. Add a little fiberfill, but keep tongue flat. Close opening with slip stitches.

23. Center tongue in mouth, with point just behind teeth. Attach rounded end to back of mouth. At pointed end, catch under layer to mouth with a few hidden stitches.

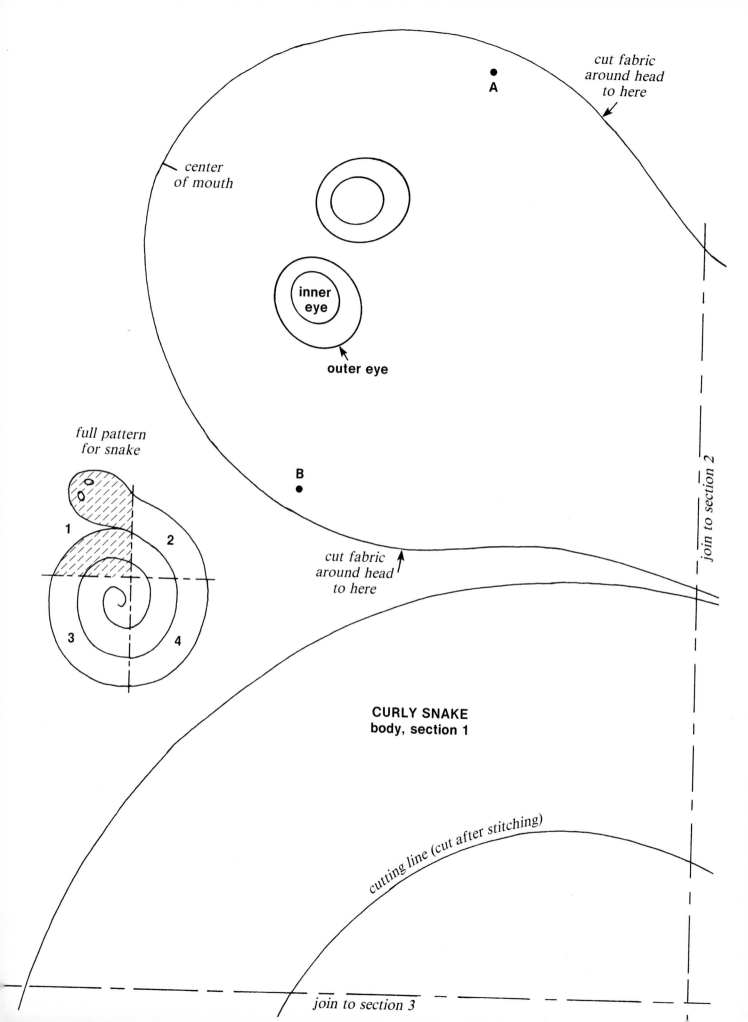

cut fabric
around head
to here

A

center
of mouth

inner
eye

outer eye

full pattern
for snake

1

2

3

4

B

cut fabric
around head
to here

join to section 2

CURLY SNAKE
body, section 1

cutting line (cut after stitching)

join to section 3

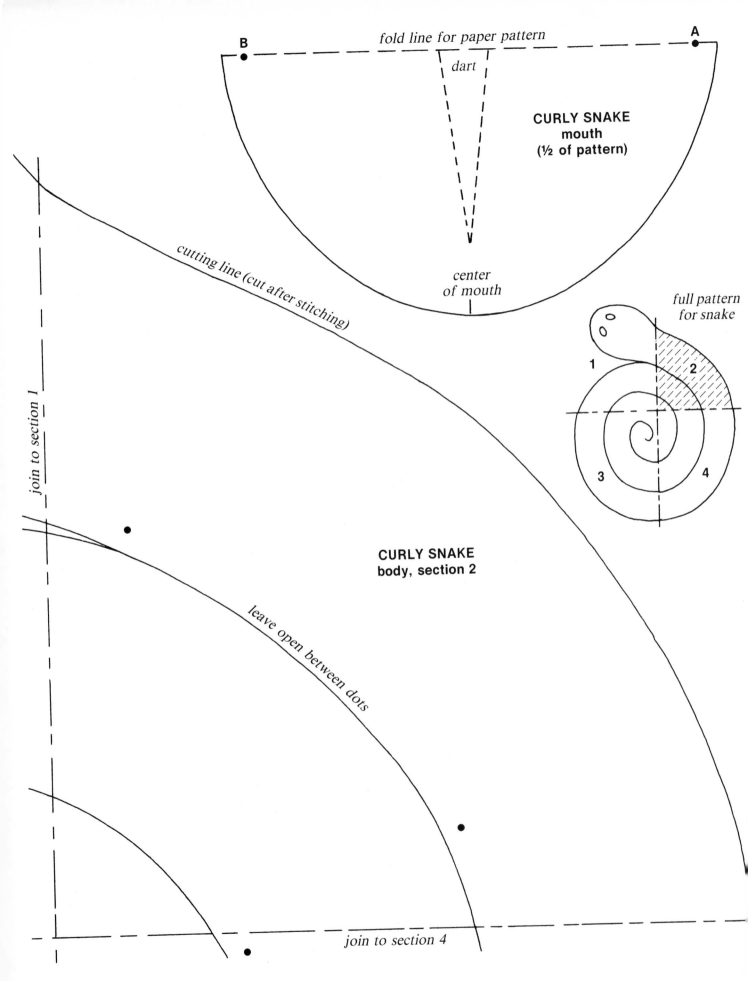

B

A

fold line for paper pattern

dart

CURLY SNAKE
mouth
(½ of pattern)

center
of mouth

cutting line (cut after stitching)

full pattern
for snake

1

2

3

4

join to section 1

leave open between dots

CURLY SNAKE
body, section 2

join to section 4

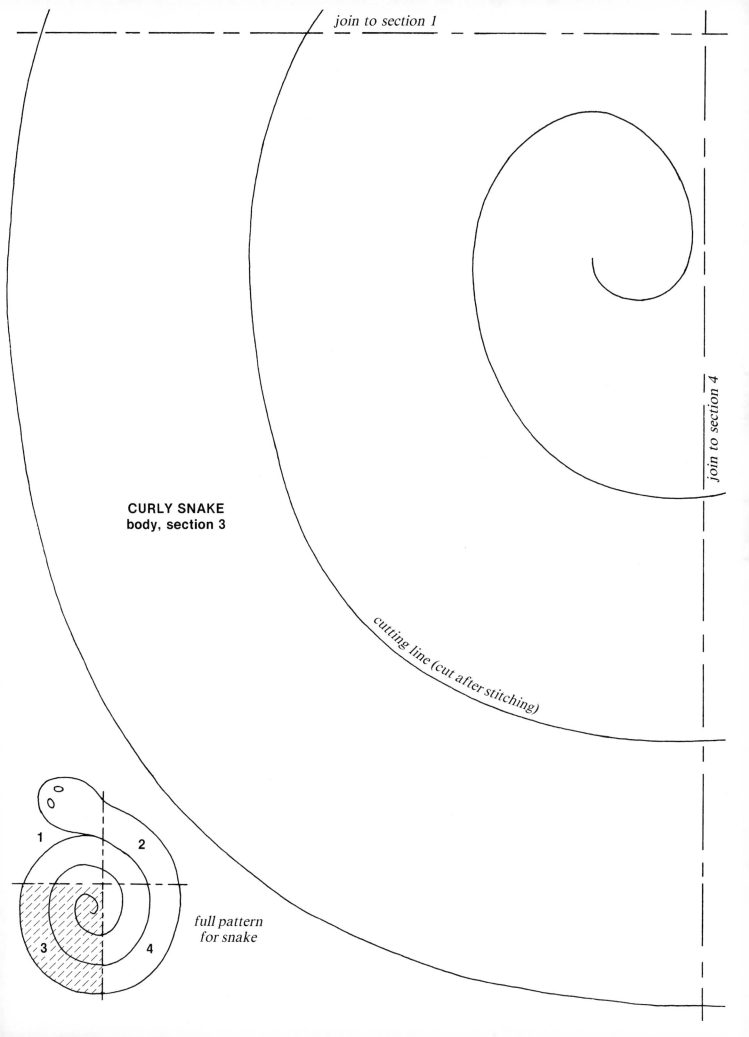

join to section 1

join to section 4

CURLY SNAKE
body, section 3

cutting line (cut after stitching)

1

2

3

4

full pattern
for snake

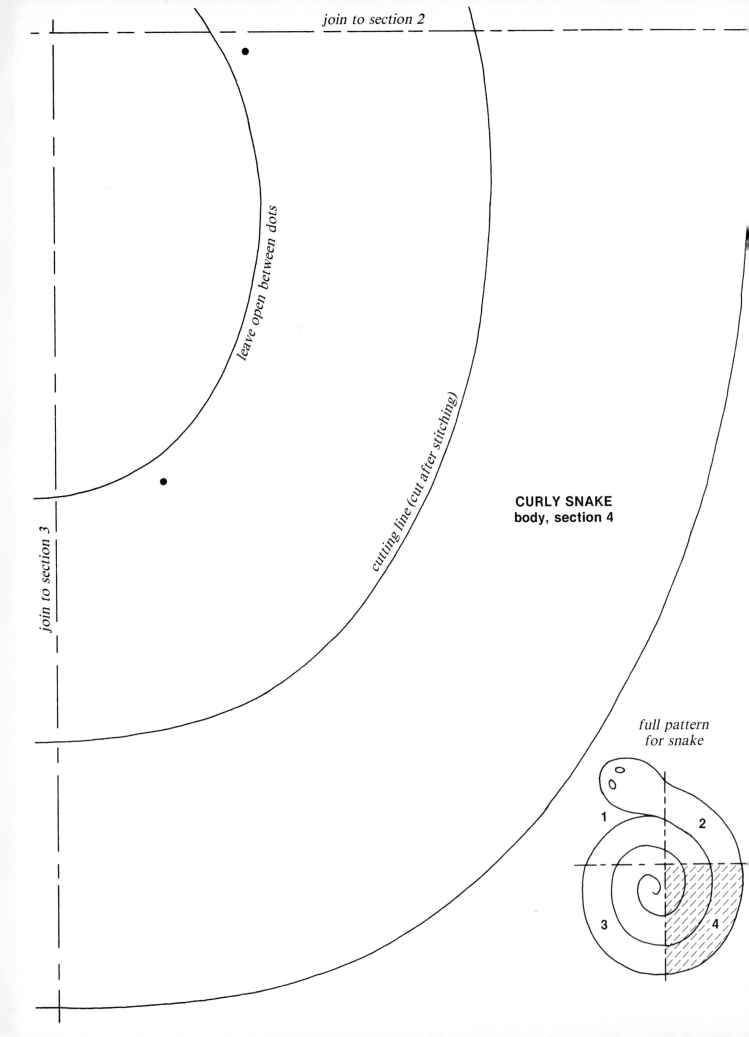

join to section 2

leave open between dots

cutting line (cut after stitching)

CURLY SNAKE
body, section 4

join to section 3

*full pattern
for snake*

1

2

3

4

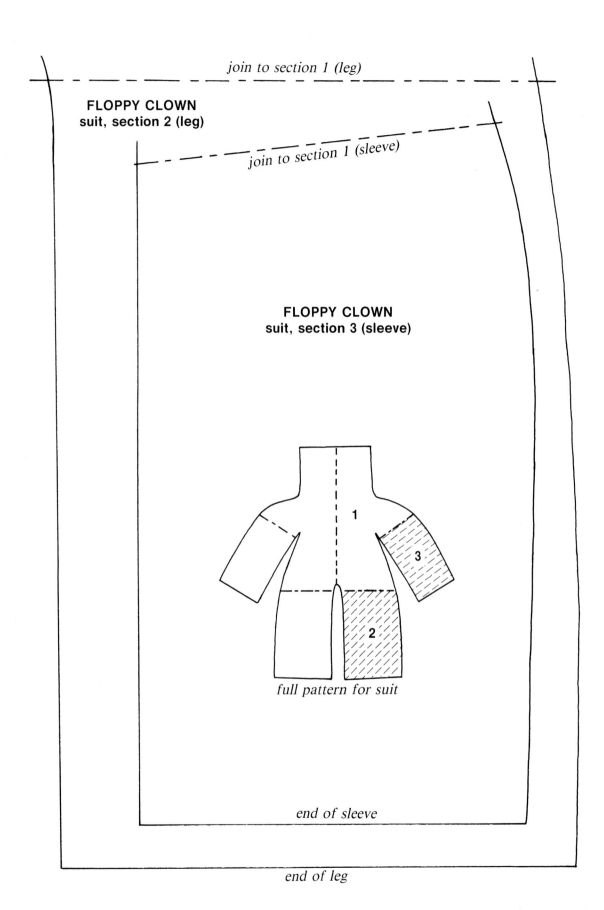

join to section 1 (leg)

**FLOPPY CLOWN
suit, section 2 (leg)**

join to section 1 (sleeve)

**FLOPPY CLOWN
suit, section 3 (sleeve)**

1

3

2

full pattern for suit

end of sleeve

end of leg

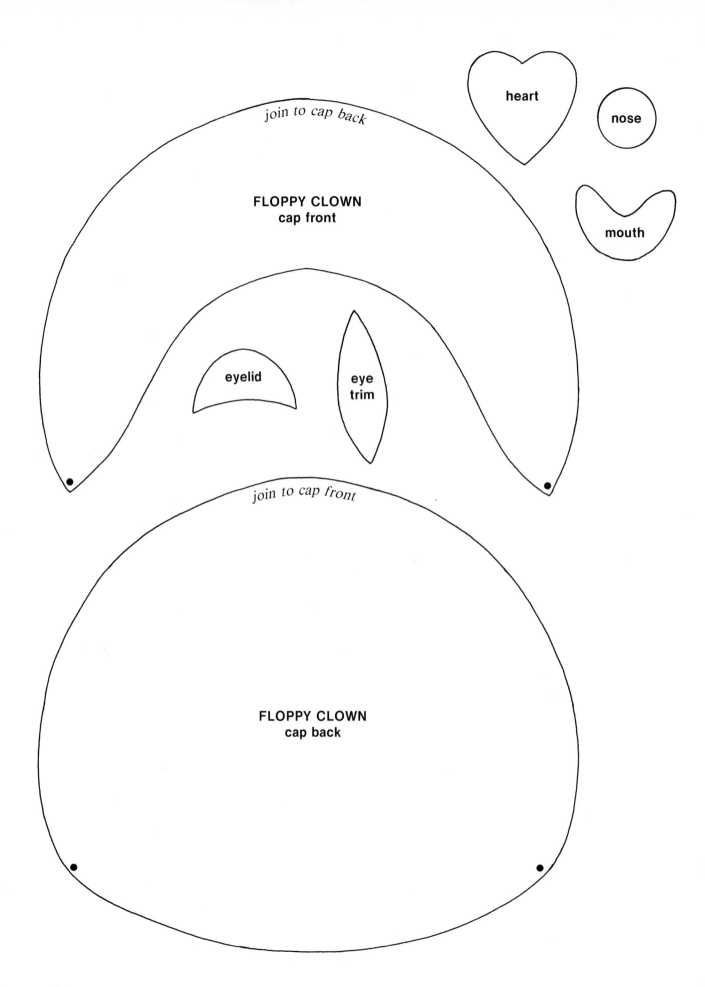

heart

nose

join to cap back

FLOPPY CLOWN
cap front

mouth

eyelid

eye
trim

join to cap front

FLOPPY CLOWN
cap back

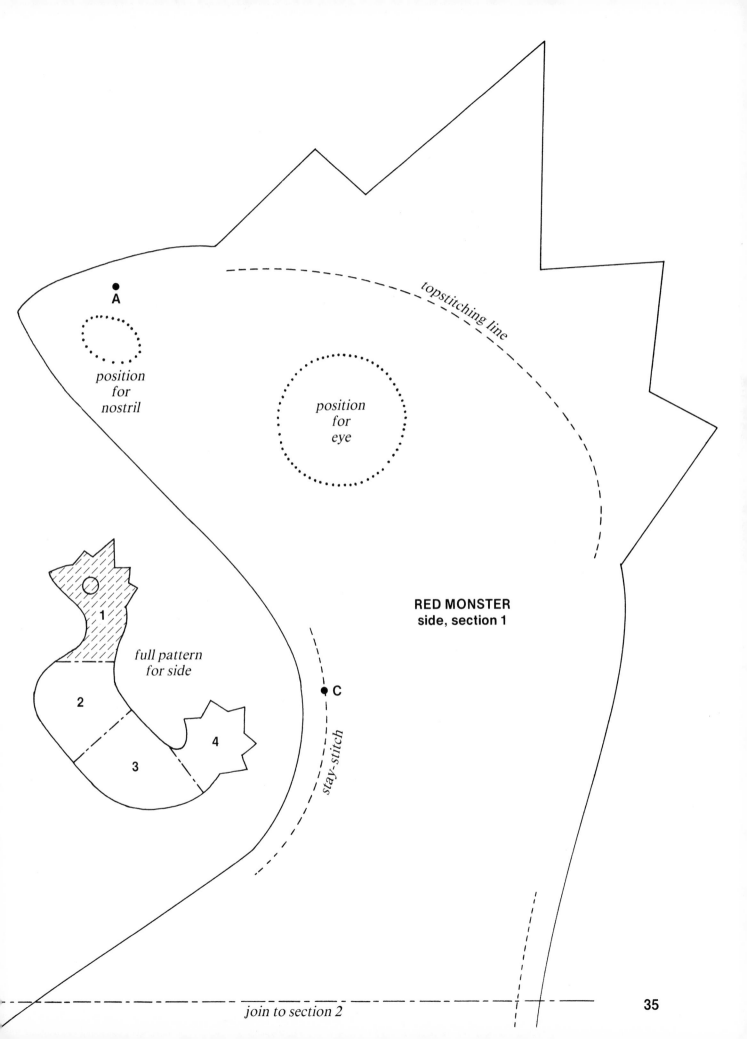

● A

*position
for
nostril*

*position
for
eye*

topstitching line

**RED MONSTER
side, section 1**

1

*full pattern
for side*

2

3

4

● C

stay-stitch

join to section 2

35

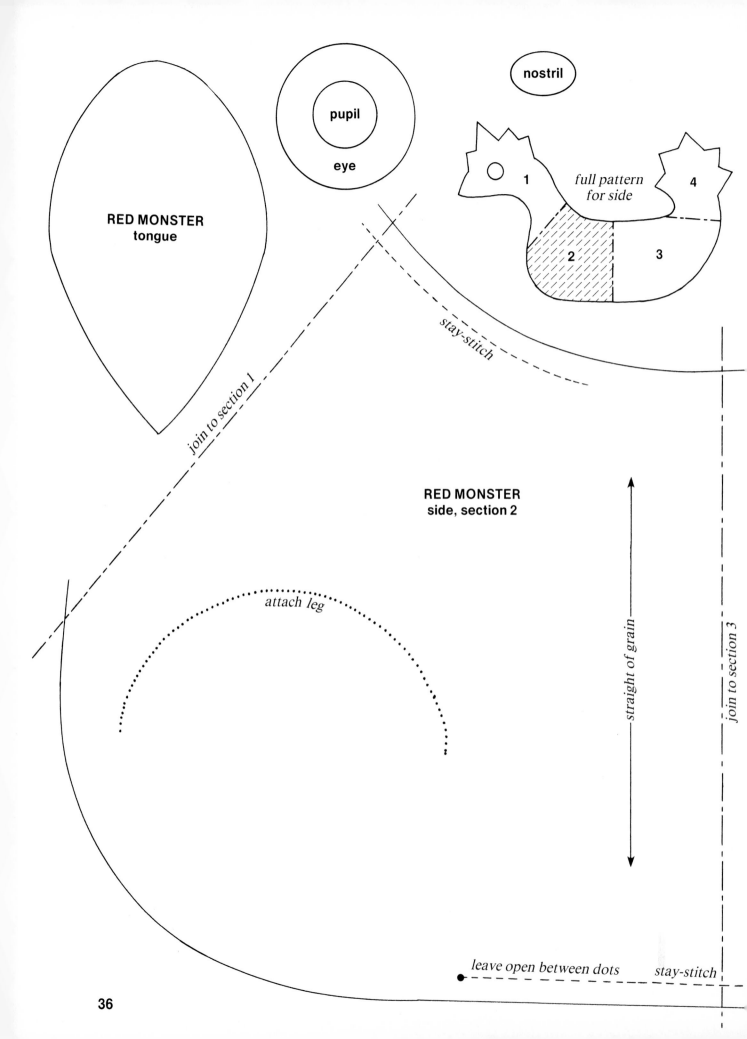

RED MONSTER
tongue

pupil

eye

nostril

1

full pattern
for side

4

2

3

stay-stitch

join to section 1

RED MONSTER
side, section 2

attach leg

straight of grain

join to section 3

leave open between dots   stay-stitch

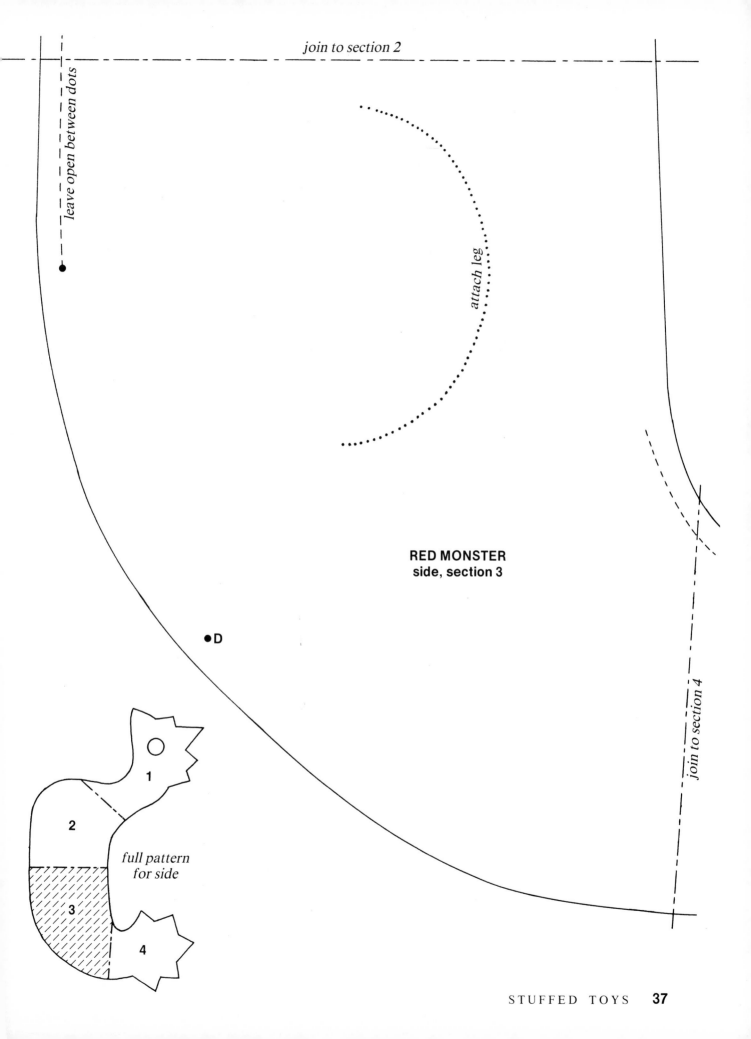

join to section 2

leave open between dots

attach leg

RED MONSTER
side, section 3

●D

join to section 4

1

2

3

4

full pattern
for side

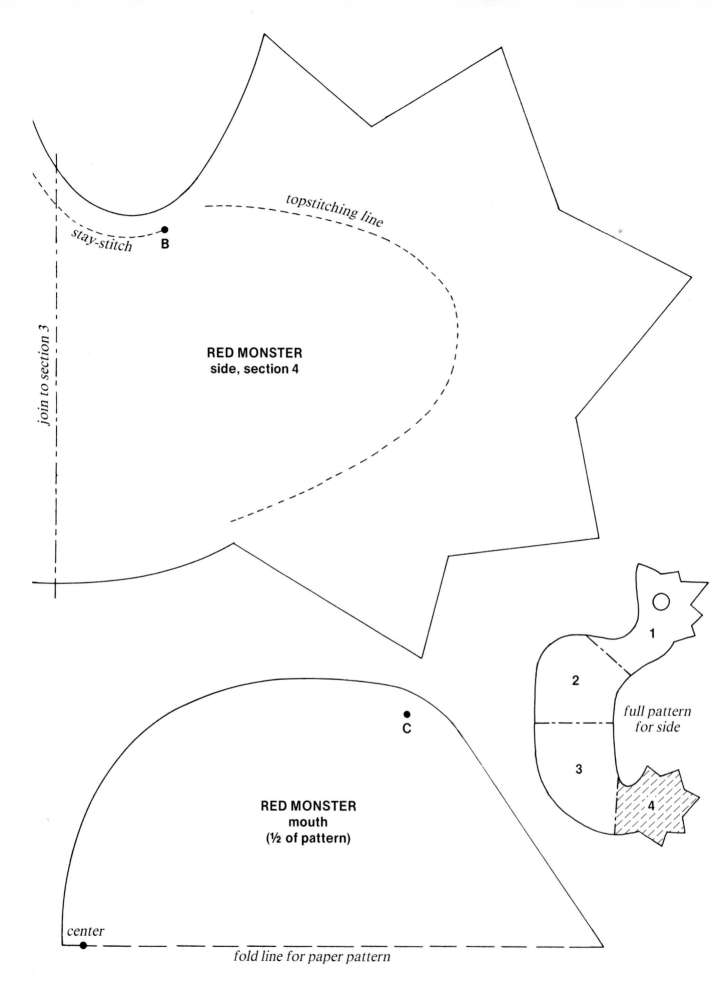

topstitching line

stay-stitch

B

join to section 3

RED MONSTER
side, section 4

C

RED MONSTER
mouth
(½ of pattern)

*full pattern
for side*

1

2

3

4

center

fold line for paper pattern

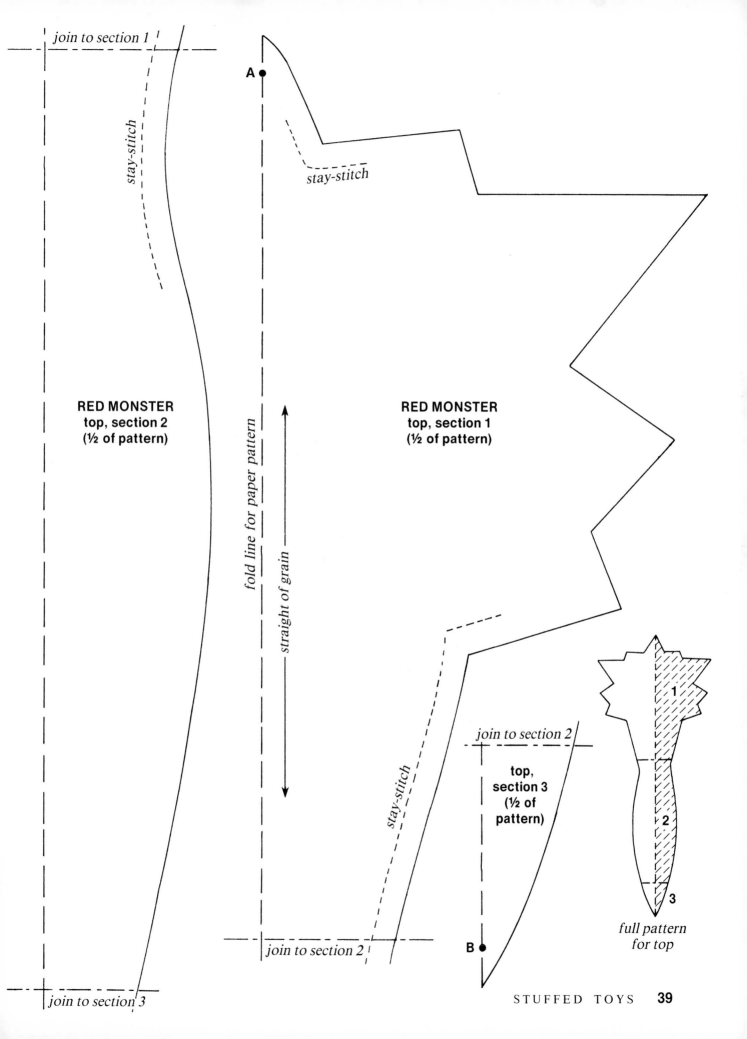

join to section 1

stay-stitch

A •

stay-stitch

RED MONSTER
top, section 2
(½ of pattern)

RED MONSTER
top, section 1
(½ of pattern)

fold line for paper pattern

straight of grain

stay-stitch

join to section 2

top,
section 3
(½ of
pattern)

join to section 2

B •

1

2

3

*full pattern
for top*

join to section 3

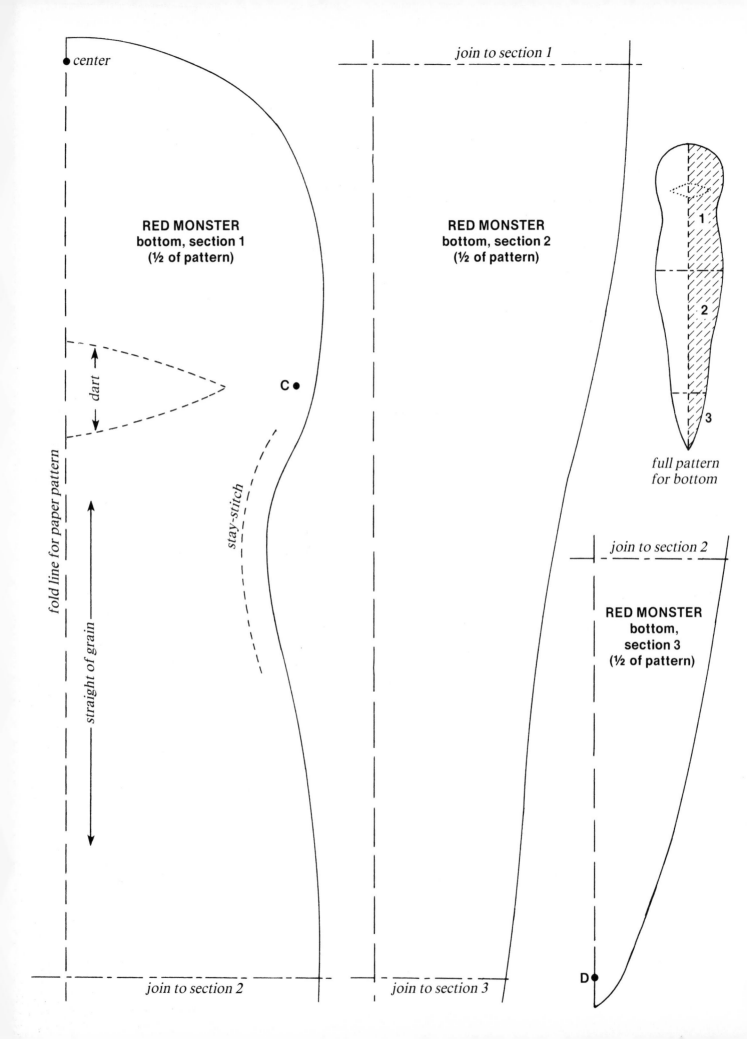

● center

RED MONSTER
bottom, section 1
(½ of pattern)

dart

fold line for paper pattern

straight of grain

stay-stitch

C ●

join to section 1

RED MONSTER
bottom, section 2
(½ of pattern)

full pattern
for bottom

1

2

3

join to section 2

RED MONSTER
bottom,
section 3
(½ of pattern)

join to section 2

join to section 3

D ●

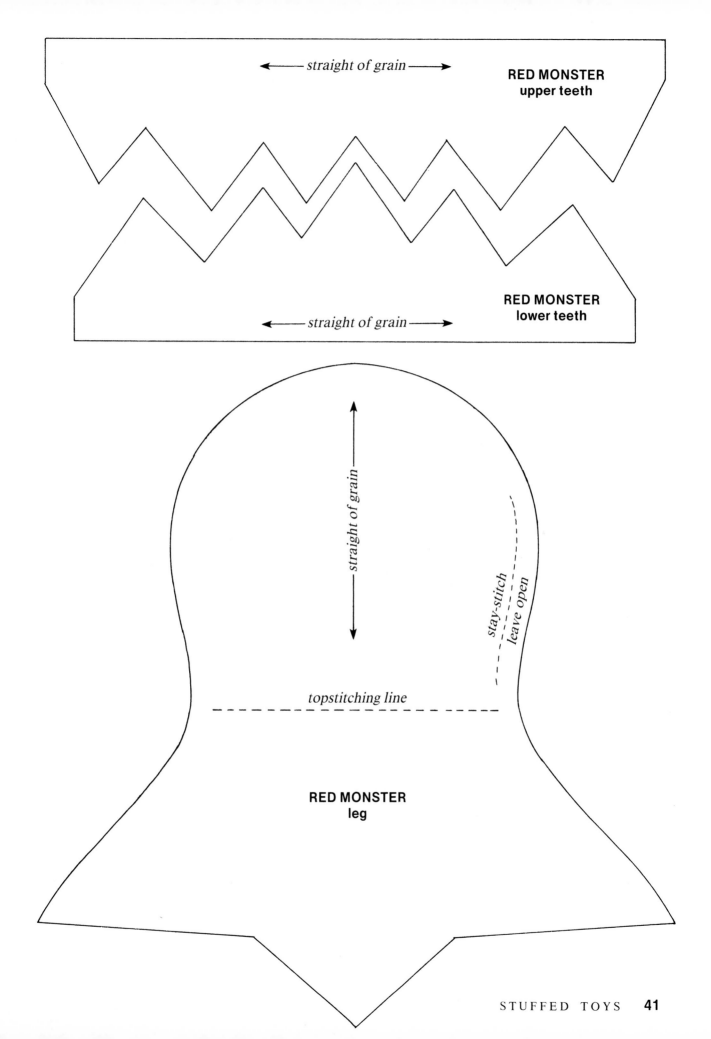

straight of grain

RED MONSTER
upper teeth

RED MONSTER
lower teeth

straight of grain

straight of grain

stay-stitch

leave open

topstitching line

RED MONSTER
leg

Purses to Wear

Wear one of these small purses when you don't want to carry a large handbag. Each of the designs is big enough to hold some money and a credit card.

The Heart Appliqué, Picture Pocket, Glad Hand and Yellow Bird have long cords that you wear around your neck.

The Sun Face Purse and the Little Pig have hidden belt guides so you can wear them on narrow belts.

Use firm, medium-weight fabrics for the outside layers, and lightweight fabrics for linings and trims. Closures are self-gripping fasteners (Velcro) that you can buy by the inch or in precut strips and circles.

GENERAL DIRECTIONS
Follow directions for each purse, referring to general guides below as needed.

To add self-gripping fastener strip
Work with purse front unit and purse back unit separately.

Keep lining pinned to purse layers along the top edges. With thread to match purse, stitch across top of each unit along fold line, ¼″ from edge. Finish raw edge with a zigzag stitch or a line of straight stitching close to the edge. Turn raw edge to wrong side along stitched line and press.

On purse front (lining side), center half of the self-gripping fastener, keeping strip just below folded edge. (Pin across the fastener to hold it in place.) Machine-stitch along each edge of fastener strip, starting and ending at raw edge of fabric.

Attach other half of fastener to purse back in same manner.

To add neck cord
Use the 33″ cord. Cut it shorter, if necessary. (Cord also can be shortened later by tying a knot in the center.)

Position one end of cord inside purse along seam, with cut end of cord 1″ from top opening. Sew cord to the seam allowance or along the seam.

Repeat with opposite end of cord on other side of purse.

To make belt guide
Use the 2x3″ rectangle. Turn each 3″ edge ¼″ to the wrong side and press. Open fabric and fold in half, matching the 2″ edges. Stitch a ¼″ seam. Press seam open with fingers, and turn tube to right side. Center seam on one side. At each end, tuck seam allowances inside and hand-stitch edges together.

HEART APPLIQUÉ NECK PURSE

(color photo, page 48)

This easy-to-make denim purse has a padded red heart added to the front.

MATERIALS
Medium-weight denim, 6x12″, for purse
Red print, 6x12″, for lining
Red fabric, 4″ square, for heart
Navy and red thread
Polyester batting, 4″ square
33″ narrow navy cord
3½″ black self-gripping fastener (cut to ³/₈″ width)

DIRECTIONS
For extra help with patterns, templates, appliqué and stitching, see *Sewing Guides*, page 1.

Cut patterns and fabric

1. Trace pattern A, page 56, and cut out. Seam allowance is included.

Also trace pattern for heart appliqué and make a template. Seam allowance will be added when cutting fabric.

2. Fold denim and red print fabrics in half, right sides inside. On top of denim, trace A (for front and back). On top of print, trace A (for lining). Cut out on pencil lines.

On right side of red fabric, trace heart template. Cut out, adding ¼″ seam allowance.

Trace heart on batting and cut out on pencil line.

Assemble purse

3. Stay-stitch around red heart, just outside pencil line. Slash seam allowance to stitching at V point and on each side of the V. Turn seam allowance to wrong side on pencil line and finger-press.

Place batting against wrong side of red heart. Turn seam allowance over batting and baste along edge.

4. Center heart appliqué on right side of purse front, with tip of heart 1″ from bottom of purse. Pin in place, and attach with a hemming stitch.

With red thread, hand-quilt heart, about ¼″ from edge.

5. Pin a lining piece to purse front, wrong sides together. Then pin a lining piece to purse back in the same way.

To add self-gripping fastener strip, follow the *General Directions.*

6. Place purse front against purse back, right sides together. Pin around outside, matching edges. Stitch from top edge, around curve to top edge on opposite side; make a ¼″ seam

and backstitch at both ends to secure. To finish seam, zigzag over raw edges or straight-stitch close to edge. Turn purse to right side.

7. To add neck cord, follow *General Directions.*

PICTURE POCKET NECK PURSE

(color photo, page 48)

Here's a way to carry a favorite person's picture—and some money—in the same purse. This could be the perfect gift for a schoolgirl.

The picture slot inside takes a regular school photo (finished size 1⅞x2½″). The flower "frame" has a 1½″ opening.

MATERIALS
Aqua medium-weight fabric, 6x12″, for purse
Bright green lightweight fabric, 6x25″, for flower and lining
Aqua and green thread
Thin polyester batting, 4″ square
33″ narrow aqua cord
3½″ beige self-gripping fastener (cut to ⅜″ width)
Small snap, ¼″ diameter, for picture slot
Photo, 1⅞x2½″

DIRECTIONS
For extra help with patterns, templates and stitching, see *Sewing Guides,* page 1.

Cut patterns and fabric

1. Trace patterns for A and picture slot, page 57, and cut out. Seam allowances are included.

Also trace pattern for flower and make a template. Seam allowance will be added when cutting fabric.

2. Fold aqua fabric in half, right side inside. On top, trace A; copy center circle and mark center point with a dot. Cut out fabric on outside pencil lines; do not cut circle.

At one end of green lining fabric, trace pattern for picture slot and cut out on pencil lines. Fold remaining green fabric to make two layers, with right side inside. On top, trace A (for lining); copy center circle and mark center point with a dot. Cut out fabric on outside pencil lines.

On the two layers of green, also trace one flower. Cut out around outside edge only, adding ¼″ seam allowance.

Assemble purse

3. Make flower. Lay green flower layers over batting square and pin. Stitch around outside curves of flower on pencil line. Trim batting close to stitching. Trim seam allowances to ⅛″, and slash to stitching at V points.

Cut out inner circle, adding ¼″ seam allowance. Turn flower to right side, work seam to edge and pin. With aqua (contrasting) thread, hand-quilt around outside edge of flower with a small running stitch, about ⅛″ from edge.

4. Add flower to purse. On purse front (top layer), transfer center point of circle to right side. Lay purse front flat, right side up. On top, center flower, right side up, over center point. Baste flower in place (Fig. 1). Place lining on top, wrong side up.

Fig. 1 *Adding flower to front*

Turn layers over and pin center point of purse to center point of lining. Match center circle lines and baste around circle, using green thread. With green thread in machine, stitch around center circle. Cut out circle, leaving a ⅛" seam allowance. Slash circle seam allowance to stitching at ¼" intervals. Open seam allowances and carefully cut away batting close to stitching.

Turn right side out, pulling lining through circle, and press. To hold lining in place, fold aqua fabric out of way; with lining side up, topstitch lining to seam allowance. Smooth lining over purse front. Press on lining side to flatten any puckers at circle. Pin lining to purse front along edges.

5. Pin remaining lining piece to purse back, wrong sides together.

To add self-gripping fastener strip, follow the *General Directions.*

6. For picture slot, fold rectangular piece of fabric in half, right side inside. Stitch along the raw edges on three sides, making a ¼" seam; leave 2" open on long side for turning. Trim corners, turn to right side and press. Close opening by hand.

7. Center rectangle over circle opening, with one short side just under fastener strip at top. Pin in place. Sew half of snap inside top edge of slot and other half to lining. By hand, sew three edges of rectangle to lining.

Insert picture to check placement. Add a few stitches at the bottom to raise the photo, if necessary.

8. To hold lining to purse front, stitch layers together around curve; keep stitching less than ¼" from edge. (Lining may not quite reach outside edge of purse at all points.)

Place purse front against purse back, right sides together. Pin around outside, matching purse layers. Stitch from top edge, around curve, to top edge on opposite side; make a ¼" seam and backstitch at both ends to secure. To finish seam, zigzag over raw edges or straight-stitch close to edge. Turn purse to right side.

9. To add neck cord, follow *General Directions.*

GLAD HAND NECK PURSE

(color photo, page 48)

The closed hand keeps your money safe. Lift the fingers to open the purse.

MATERIALS
Red medium-weight fabric, 9x11", for purse
Red lightweight print, 5x10", for lining
Red and black thread
Thin polyester batting, 6½x8"
33" thin red cord
2 red self-gripping fasteners, ¾" circles

DIRECTIONS
For extra help with patterns, templates and stitching, see *Sewing Guides,* page 1.

Cut patterns and fabric
1. Trace pattern pieces for hand, page 58, and for lining, page 56. Make templates for all pattern pieces. Seam allowances will be added when cutting fabric.

2. Place templates, face down, on wrong side of fabric and trace outlines. On red, trace one full hand, one upper hand and one lower hand; leave room for ¼" seam allowances. Mark dots for fold lines, but do not copy topstitching lines.

Fold lining fabric in half, right side inside. On top, trace lining.

Cut out fabric, adding ¼" seam allowances.

Place full hand pattern on batting and cut out around shape, adding about ¼" seam allowance.

Assemble purse

3. Fold upper and lower hand pieces to wrong side along fold (pencil) lines and press. (Remember to keep the folds open when stitching.)

4. Stack layers and stitch (Fig. 2). Pin upper hand to full hand, right sides together; keep upper hand on top. Match pencil lines and dots at ends of fold line. Lay pinned layers over batting and pin in a few places to hold.

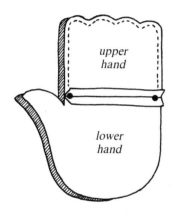

Fig. 2 *Stitching layers together*

Stitch along pencil line from one dot at fold line, around top of hand to opposite dot; do not stitch beyond dots. Then pin raw edge up (out of the way) along fold.

5. Place lower hand against full hand, right sides together, and pin. (Unpin batting in this area.) Match pencil lines, dots at ends of fold line, and V point at thumb. (Fold lines on upper and lower sections will butt together.)

Pin layers over batting. Check batting side to be sure stitching on lower hand will begin and end where stitching

on upper hand left off; use pins to mark exact dot positions.

With fold open, stitch from dot to dot.

6. Trim batting close to stitching. Trim seam allowances to under ¼". Slash seam allowances to stitching line at V points between fingers and at thumb. Slash inside curve along thumb and trim tip of thumb.

Turn to right side, working seams to edge. Let raw edge of upper hand lie flat inside pocket; fold raw edge of lower hand to inside of pocket. Press both sides of purse lightly.

7. Mark topstitching lines. Place paper pattern for full hand over matching fabric piece; mark straight lines between fingers and curved lines for fingernails. Place pattern for lower hand over matching fabric piece; mark straight line by thumb and mark curve for thumbnail.

8. For topstitching, use regular black thread in the machine and a small stitch. Leave at least 4″ of thread at both ends of the seam; do not backstitch to secure.

With pocket side up, stitch line at thumb. Then stitch thumbnail. With full hand up, stitch between fingers (do not catch fold on underside).

To secure threads at each end of stitching lines, tie the two strands in a knot. Thread the strands in a needle, insert needle at end of stitching, work needle through batting for about 1″ and bring it up along stitching line. Tug thread gently and clip close to fabric.

Finally, stitch one continuous line for fingernails. Secure thread ends as above.

9. To add neck cord, follow *General Directions.*

Add lining and finish

10. Stitch the two print layers, right sides together; leave top edge open. Turn top edge ¼" to wrong side and press.

Slip lining inside pocket and sew in place by hand.

11. To add closure, use thin half of fasteners on upper hand. Position one circle at the tip of the third finger and another on the fourth finger. Sew in place, catching upper hand and batting only.

Position matching circle sections on lower hand and sew in place.

YELLOW BIRD NECK PURSE

(color photo, page 48)

This big yellow bird has a handy pocket under its wing.

MATERIALS

Yellow medium-weight fabric, 9x16″, for bird
Blue lightweight fabric, 6½x16″, for wing and lining
Thin polyester batting, 9″ square, for padding
33″ thin yellow cord
Beige self-gripping fastener, ¾″ circle
Yellow, blue and beige thread

DIRECTIONS

For extra help with patterns, templates and stitching, see *Sewing Guides,* page 1.

Cut patterns and fabric

1. Trace pattern pieces for bird and lining, page 59, and make templates. Seam allowances will be added when cutting fabric.

2. Fold each fabric in half, right side inside. On yellow, trace body and flap, face up. On blue, trace wing and pocket lining, face up. Cut out, adding ¼" seam allowances.

Assemble purse

3. For flap, stitch yellow layers around curve, right sides together; begin at top raw edge (above A), follow pencil line and end at raw edge above B. Trim seam allowance along curve to ⅛", and slash seam allowance at inside curve. Turn flap to right side and press lightly.

4. Position flap on top layer of body (this will be the back of bird), right sides together; match dots A and B, and pin (Fig. 3). With body piece on top, stitch on pencil line across straight edge between dots. Trim ends of seam allowance on flap, and pin flap away from seam line at tail.

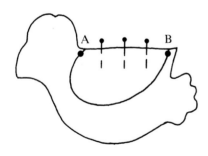

Fig. 3 *Adding flap*

5. To join body layers, place stitched layer over bottom layer, right sides together (flap is in the middle and pencil lines are on top). Pin layers together. Then pin bird to a 6x9" layer of batting.

Begin at dot A on neck and stitch on pencil line around bird, ending at raw edge above dot B. Trim batting close to stitching and along top raw edge. Trim seam allowance along stitching to under ¼", and slash seam allowance at V points and inside curves.

Turn bird to right side and press lightly (batting will be against front of bird). Press flap up, with seam allowances inside pocket.

To hold batting and front layer together, machine-stitch ¼" from pocket edge; begin and end 1" from ends of opening. Trim batting close to stitching line. Fold raw edge of pocket to inside to align with stitching on flap. Baste and press.

Fold flap over front layer along seam, and press.

6. On front of bird, use paper pattern to mark face and trim lines. Embroider eye, using two strands of blue floss and a satin stitch.

7. For other trim lines, use machine stitching. Leave at least 4" of thread at each end of the stitching lines; do not backstitch.

With yellow thread, machine-stitch line behind neck. With blue thread, stitch lines at head, beak, back and feet.

To secure threads at each end of stitching lines, tie the two strands in a knot. Thread the strands in a needle, insert needle at end of stitching, work needle through batting for about 1" and bring it up along stitching line. Tug thread gently and clip close to fabric.

8. To add neck cord, follow *General Directions.*

At head end of bird, stitch cord to back layer along neck seam.

Add lining and finish

9. Pin blue lining pieces, right sides together. Stitch curve on pencil line, beginning and ending at top raw edge.

Turn top edge ¼" to wrong side (outside) and press.

Tuck lining inside pocket, with A and B in correct position. Pin and hand-stitch in place.

10. To add closure, use thin half of fastener on flap. Position circle on inside edge of flap. Sew in place by hand, catching both layers of flap (stitches will be covered by the wing).

Position matching circle section on body and sew in place.

11. To make wing, keep wing layers right sides together, and pin over layer of batting. Stitch around wing, leaving 2" open along top for turning. Trim batting close to stitching and along seam line on open area. Trim seam allowances to ⅛" around curved edge.

Turn wing to right side and press lightly. Close opening with slip stitches.

For trim, use yellow thread and machine-stitch around wing, ⅜" from outside edge. Stitch a second trim line, ⅜" from first line. Pull threads to back of wing. Tie and hide thread ends as in Step 7.

12. Position wing on flap (wing will extend beyond flap along curved edge). Sew flap to wing along curve and across top, catching under layer of wing only.

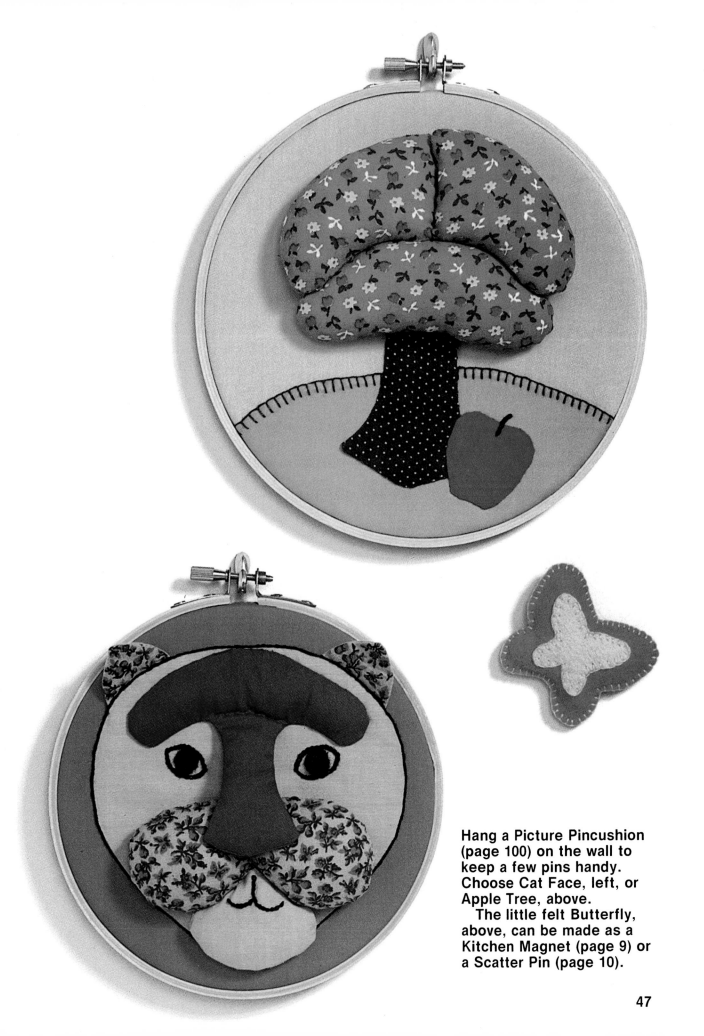

Hang a Picture Pincushion (page 100) on the wall to keep a few pins handy. Choose Cat Face, left, or Apple Tree, above.

The little felt Butterfly, above, can be made as a Kitchen Magnet (page 9) or a Scatter Pin (page 10).

47

Purses to Wear (page 42) have a cord to hang around your neck or a belt guide to slip over a belt. Shown clockwise from below are Sun Face, Little Pig, Heart Appliqué, Picture Pocket, Glad Hand and Yellow Bird.

Round Spider Web Shoulder
Bag (page 62) has its own
felt spider. Multicolor
Shoulder Bag (page 64) can
be made in solid colors or
in prints.

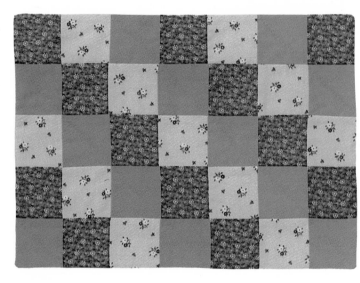

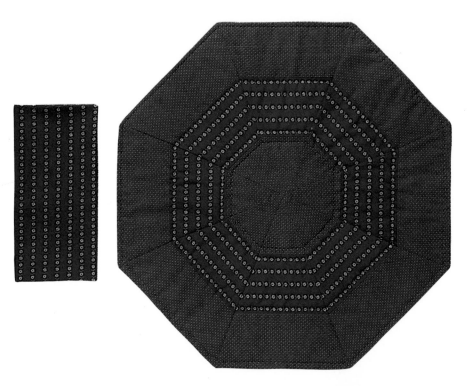

Use a shortcut method to stitch these three Pieced Placemats (page 91). Shown top to bottom are Square Steps, Eight Triangles and Christmas Placemat.

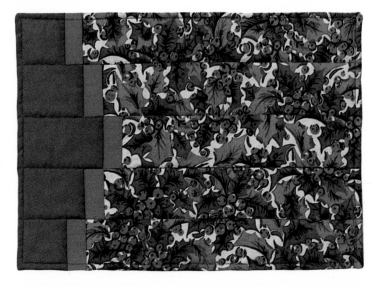

SUN FACE BELT PURSE

(color photo, page 48)

Use contrasting binding to finish the edges of this simple 6x7" purse. Add a smiling sun face to the front and two belt guides to the back.

MATERIALS

Green medium-weight fabric, 9½x15", for purse
Green lightweight print, 9½x15", for lining
Yellow fabric scraps, for sun
Thin polyester batting, 9½x15", for padding
1 yd. bright blue polyester knitted binding
Beige self-gripping fastener, ¾" circle
Thread to match fabric, binding and fastener
Black embroidery floss

DIRECTIONS

For extra help with patterns, templates and stitching, see *Sewing Guides,* page 1.

Cut patterns and fabric

1. Trace pattern pieces for purse, pages 60-61, and cut out. Seam allowances are included.

Also trace pattern pieces for sun face A and back circle, and make templates. Seam allowances will be added when cutting fabric.

2. Place pattern pieces for purse on wrong side of green solid and green print. On each fabric, trace one flap/back and one front. Trace same pieces on batting. Cut out all pieces on pencil lines.

On green solid, mark two rectangles (belt guides), 2x3" each. (This size fits a belt ½-¾" wide. For a wider belt, add to the 2" measure.) Cut out on pencil lines.

Assemble purse

3. Place flap/back lining piece right side down. Add layer of batting. On top, place green layer, right side up. Pin layers together. To hold in place, use green thread and machine-stitch layers along edge; use a zigzag stitch if your machine has one.

Repeat steps to stack and stitch front pieces.

4. To make belt guides, follow *General Directions.* Make two guides.

5. Position each belt guide on purse back, ½" below fold line and ½" from center point on pattern. Attach top and bottom edges with machine zigzag or straight stitches.

6. Add binding. On front layers, pin binding along top, enclosing raw edge. Hand-stitch one edge of binding to the outside fabric and one edge to the lining.

Position purse front against the flap/back, lining sides together. To hold layers in place, pin and straight-stitch along the edge by machine.

Pin binding around raw edges of purse, beginning 1" from center front of flap. Hand-stitch one edge of binding to fabric. Where binding meets on flap, trim binding, turn raw edge under and hem. Then hand-stitch other edge of binding in place.

7. To add closure, use thin half of fastener on flap. Position circle against inside of flap, close to binding. With beige thread, sew in place; catch all layers.

Position other half of the fastener on purse front and sew in place.

8. To make sun face, stack two 4" squares of yellow fabric, right sides together. On top, place sun template A and trace outline. Then use paper pattern on fabric to mark inner circle. Lift top layer of fabric. In center of circle, carefully make two 1" cuts to form a cross (for turning to right side after stitching).

Place yellow layers over a 4" square of batting and pin. With small stitches, machine-stitch around sunrays; at the end of each point, take a small stitch across tip.

Trim batting close to stitching. Cut fabric, leaving ⅛" seam allowances; clip V points to stitching. Turn sun to right side through cut crosslines. Work seam to edge and press lightly.

On right side (uncut center), mark face and circle. With two strands of black floss, embroider eyes and mouth with a stem stitch. With thread to match fabric, machine-stitch around circle.

To make back, trace circle template on right side of yellow fabric. Cut out, adding ⅛" seam allowance. Turn seam allowance to wrong side and baste. Position circle over back of sun to cover slashes, and hand-stitch in place.

9. Position sun on purse flap, covering the stitches on fastener and the seam on binding. Sew in place with hidden stitches.

LITTLE PIG BELT PURSE

(color photo, page 48)

Lift the pig's face and you find the hidden pocket. A belt guide is stitched to the back.

MATERIALS

Tan medium-weight
  fabric, 9½x15″, for pig
Brown lightweight fabric,
  9½x13″, for lining
Thin polyester batting,
  5x6″, for padding face
Beige self-gripping
  fastener, ¾″ circle
Thread to match fabric
  and fastener
Black embroidery floss

DIRECTIONS

Stitch ¼″ seams. For extra help with patterns, templates and stitching, see *Sewing guides,* page 1.

Cut patterns and fabric

1. Trace pattern pieces for pig, pages 53-56, and make templates. Seam allowances are included.

2. On wrong side of tan fabric, trace face/back piece, front and two ears. Also mark a 2x3″ rectangle for belt guide. (This fits a belt ½-¾″ wide. For a wider belt, add to the 2″ measure.) Cut out on pencil lines.

On wrong side of brown lining fabric, trace one face lining, two pocket linings and two ears. Cut out on pencil lines.

On batting, trace pattern for face lining and cut out.

Assemble purse

3. On right side of face/back piece, use paper pattern to mark lines for face. On right side of front piece, use pattern to mark hoof lines.

Embroider face and hooves with two strands of black floss. Use a stem stitch for snout and hoof lines, and a satin stitch for nostrils and eyes.

4. To make belt guide follow *General Directions.*

5. Center guide on back of pig, ½″ below fold line. Attach top and bottom edges with machine zigzag or straight stitches.

6. On tan front, turn fabric to wrong side along fold line and press. Repeat with brown face lining. (Remember to keep folds open when stitching.)

7. Stack layers and stitch (Fig. 4). Place face/back piece flat, right side up, with face portion over batting. On top, place face lining, right side down. Pin layers together, matching dots at ends of fold line. Stitch around curve, from dot to dot; do not stitch beyond dots. Then pin straight edge up (out of the way) along fold.

Position front piece against face/back piece, right sides together. Pin, matching dots at ends of fold line. (Fold lines on face lining and front piece will butt together.)

Stitch around curve and hooves, from dot to dot.

8. Trim batting on head section close to stitching. Trim seam allowances along stitched seams to under ¼″, and slash to stitching in V points at hooves.

Turn face lining and front piece to right side, work seams to edge and press lightly. Fold raw edge of front piece to inside, and let raw edge of face lining lie flat inside pocket. Hand-stitch face lining to batting just below fold line.

9. On face, hand-quilt around snout, close to embroidery line; use tan thread and a short running stitch.

Add lining and finish

10. To make lining, pin pocket lining pieces, right sides together. Stitch around curve. Then stitch a second line just outside first line. Trim seam allowance to about ⅛″.

Turn top edge ¼″ to wrong side (outside) and press. Tuck lining into pocket. Pin in place and hand-stitch to top edge on front and along fold line on face lining.

11. To add closure, use thin half of fastener on flap. Position circle on face lining under snout. With beige thread, sew to lining and batting; do not catch face layer.

Position other half of fastener on body front and sew in place.

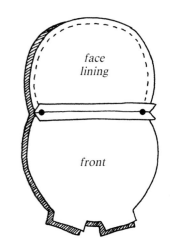

Fig. 4 *Stitching layers together*

12. To make ears, pin each tan piece to a lining piece, right sides together. Stitch around curve, leaving straight edge open. Trim seam allowance to 1/8″ and clip across point. Turn to right side and press lightly.

Turn straight edge of ear to inside, press and pin. Hand-stitch edges together.

Make a 1/4″ tuck at the center of each ear. (Turn tucks in opposite directions, so each ear will have tuck facing outside edge of body.) Catch tuck in place with a few hand stitches.

13. Position ears on pig, with a curved edge of each ear along outside edge of body, and straight edge 1/4″ below fold line. Hand-stitch straight edge of each ear to purse.

Fold each ear onto face, with tip of ear even with eyes. Catch in place with hidden stitches.

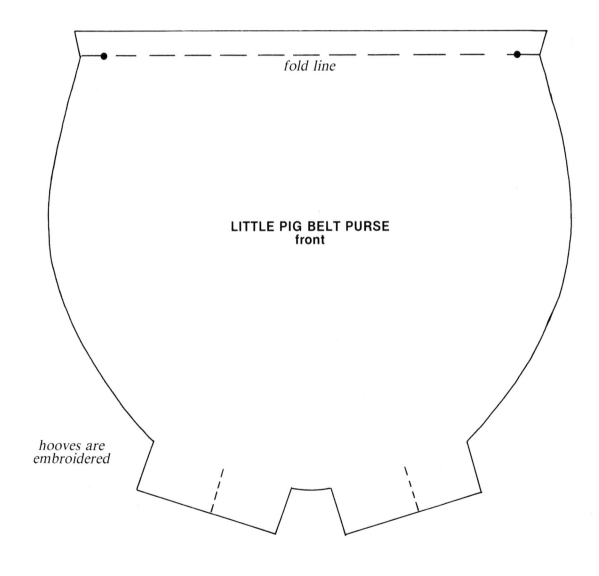

fold line

LITTLE PIG BELT PURSE
front

hooves are
embroidered

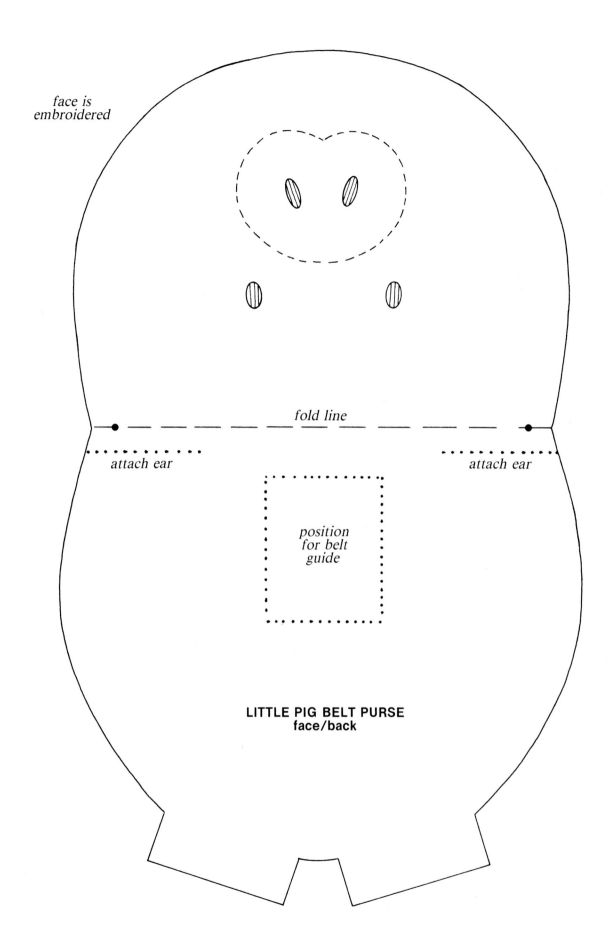

face is
embroidered

fold line

attach ear

attach ear

position
for belt
guide

LITTLE PIG BELT PURSE
face/back

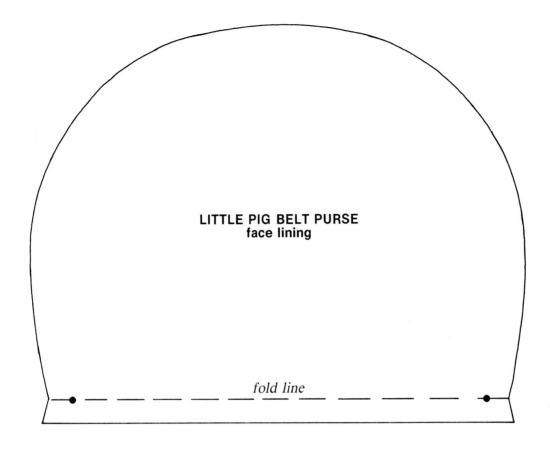

LITTLE PIG BELT PURSE
face lining

fold line

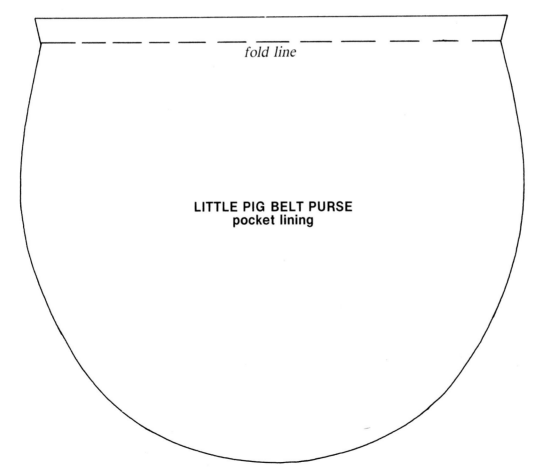

fold line

LITTLE PIG BELT PURSE
pocket lining

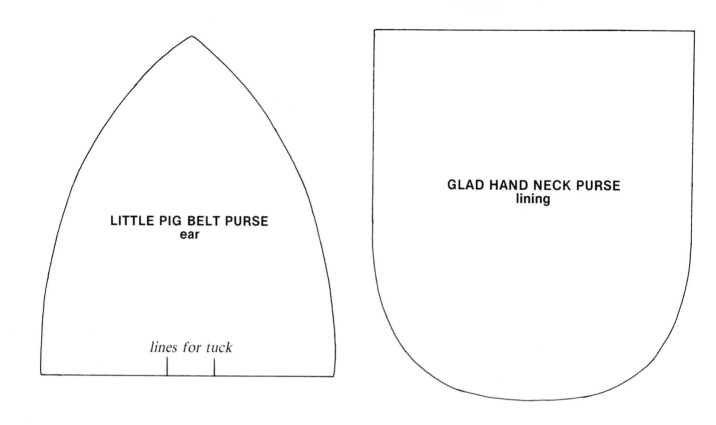

LITTLE PIG BELT PURSE
ear

lines for tuck

GLAD HAND NECK PURSE
lining

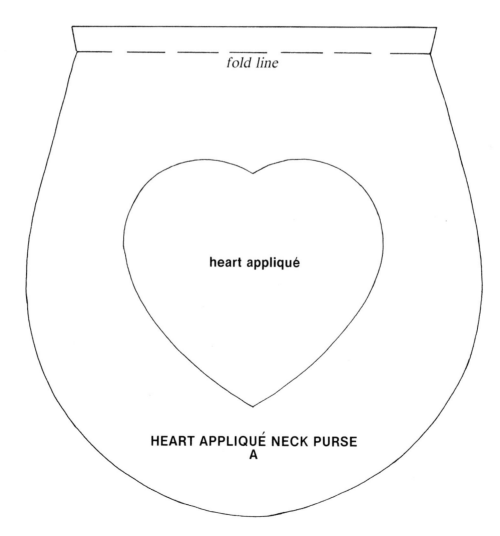

fold line

heart appliqué

HEART APPLIQUÉ NECK PURSE
A

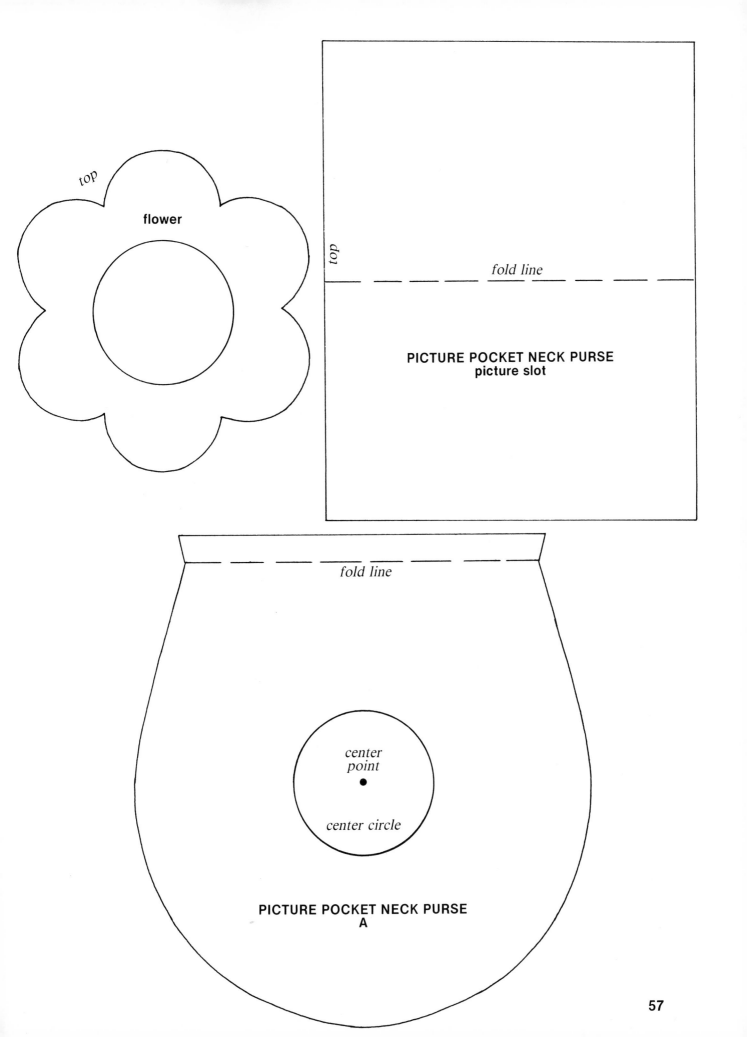

top

flower

top

fold line

PICTURE POCKET NECK PURSE
picture slot

fold line

*center
point*

center circle

PICTURE POCKET NECK PURSE
A

57

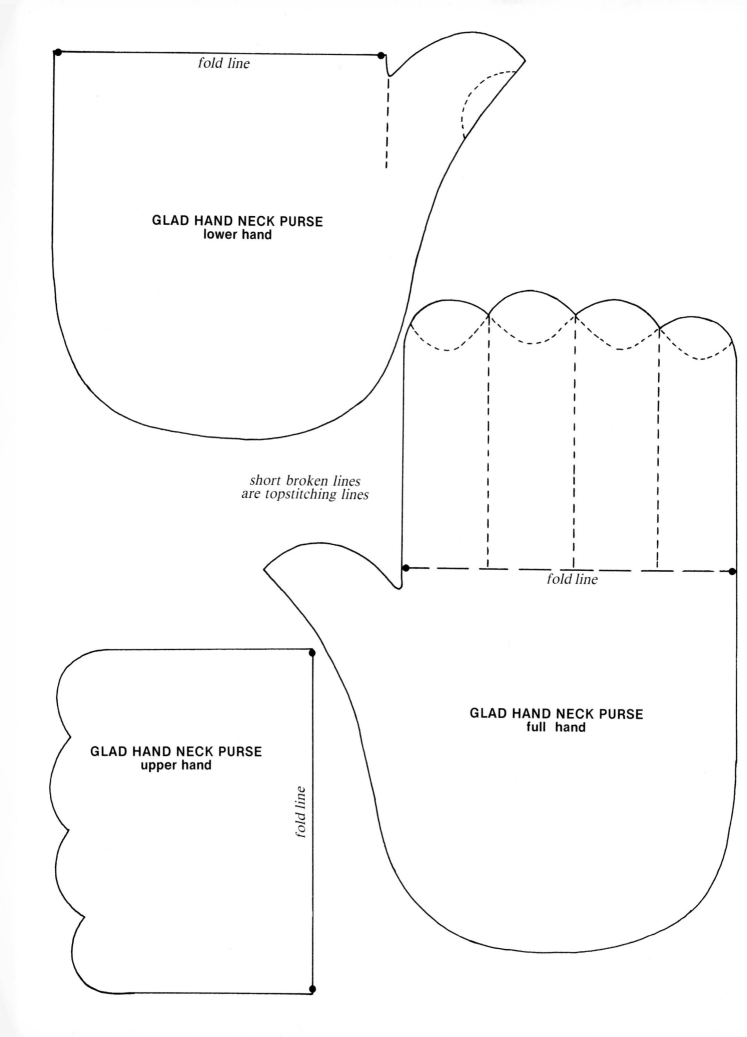

fold line

GLAD HAND NECK PURSE
lower hand

short broken lines
are topstitching lines

fold line

GLAD HAND NECK PURSE
upper hand

fold line

GLAD HAND NECK PURSE
full hand

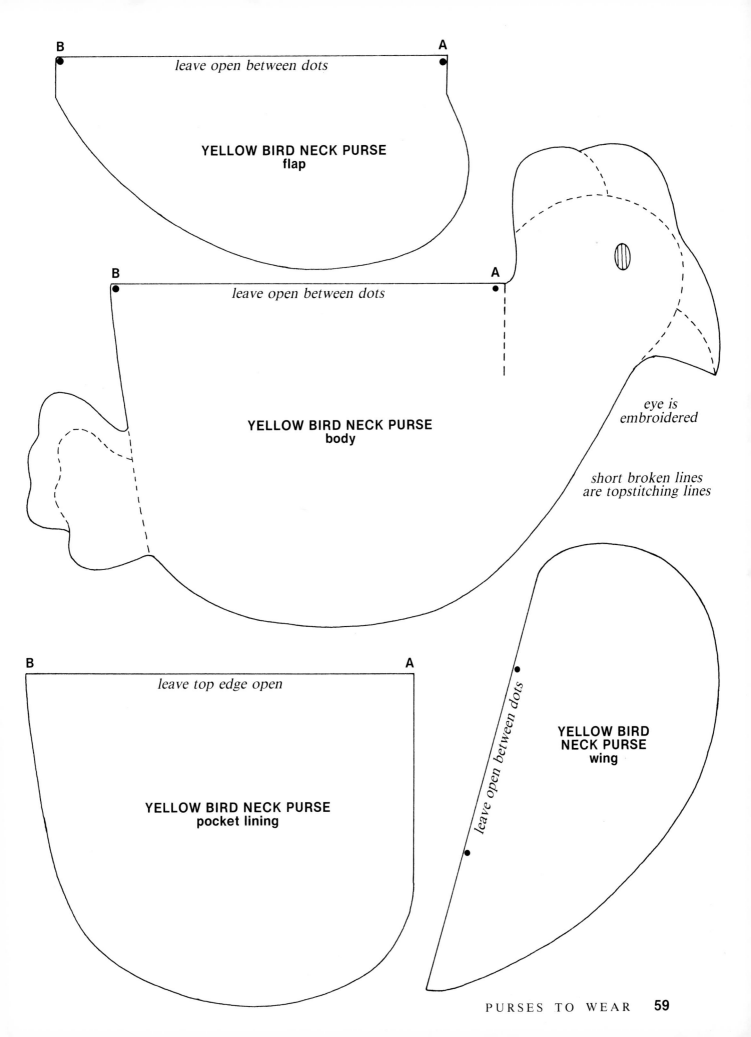

B   A

leave open between dots

YELLOW BIRD NECK PURSE
flap

B   A

leave open between dots

YELLOW BIRD NECK PURSE
body

eye is embroidered

short broken lines are topstitching lines

B   A

leave top edge open

YELLOW BIRD NECK PURSE
pocket lining

YELLOW BIRD NECK PURSE
wing

leave open between dots

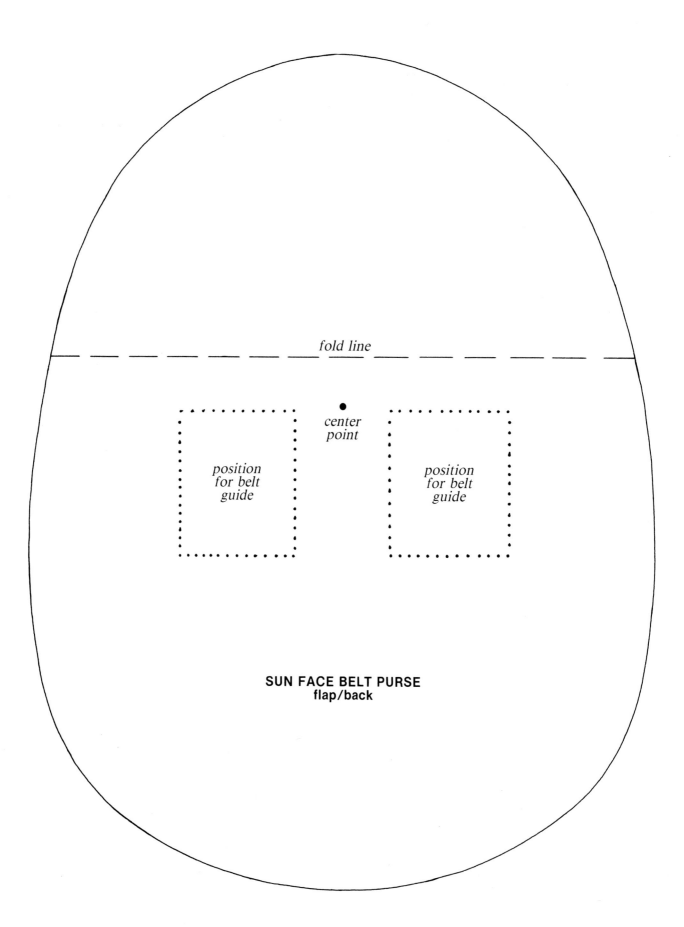

fold line

center
point

position
for belt
guide

position
for belt
guide

SUN FACE BELT PURSE
flap/back

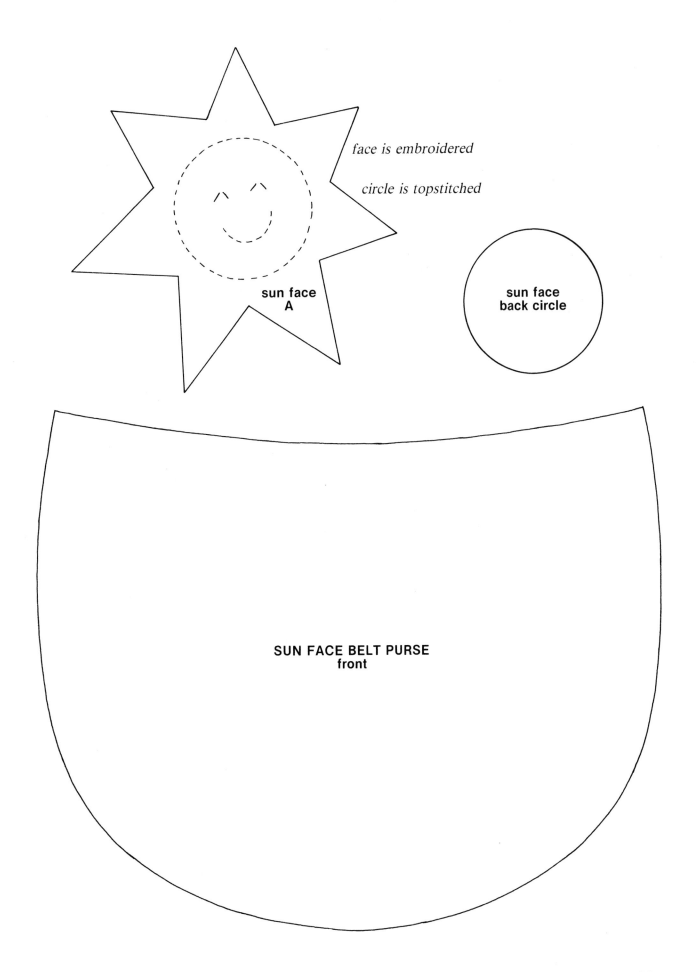

face is embroidered

circle is topstitched

sun face
A

sun face
back circle

SUN FACE BELT PURSE
front

Shoulder Bags

These novelty bags can add color and design to any outfit. The Multicolor Bag is pieced, using four different colors in solids or prints. The round Spider Web Bag has a yellow felt spider guarding its machine-stitched web.

The bags are medium size, but they're large enough to carry the essentials. Wear the long cords over your shoulder, or knot them for hand-carrying.

Both bags have zipper closings. Interfacing adds firmness to help bags keep their shapes, and a layer of batting gives them a soft look.

SPIDER WEB SHOULDER BAG

(color photo, page 49)

Stitch the lacy spider web by machine, using crochet cotton in the bobbin. Then add a smiling yellow felt spider for trim. The 9″ bag has a 2″ boxing strip between the front and back circles.

MATERIALS
⅓ yd. blue medium-weight fabric, 44″ wide, for bag
⅓ yd. blue lightweight print, 44″ wide, for lining
Muslin (or other white lightweight fabric), 12″ square, for backing front
12″ blue zipper
Blue and yellow thread
Yellow crochet cotton (DMC No. 8 or similar weight), for stitching web
Thin polyester batting, 18x25″
Fusible non-woven interfacing (for medium-weight fabric): one strip 2½x18½″; two strips, 1x12½″ each
2 lengths narrow blue cord: 1 piece 44″ and 1 piece 42″
Yellow felt scraps, for spider
4 lengths yellow chenille stems, 4″ each, for spider
Blue and yellow embroidery floss
Polyester fiberfill

DIRECTIONS
For extra help with patterns, templates and stitching, see *Sewing Guides,* page 1.

Cut patterns and fabric
1. Trace full circle pattern for bag, pages 65-66, joining sections on broken lines. Go over inside lines with a pen to make them darker. Cut out circle. Also trace pattern for spider and make a template. Seam allowances are included.
2. On wrong side of blue fabric, trace two circles (a front and back); mark top of bag. Also measure and mark three boxing strips: one strip 2½x18½″, and two strips, 1⅜x12½″ each. Cut out on pencil lines.

On wrong side of print fabric, trace two circles (a front and back). Also mark three boxing strips: one strip 2½x18½″, and two strips, 1¼x12½″ each. Cut out on pencil lines.

Place all lining pieces over batting (two circles, three boxing strips) and cut out matching pieces.

On muslin, trace circle pattern. Then place fabric over pattern, matching circle lines. Tape layers together and trace spider web. Remove pattern and cut out fabric circle on pencil line.

Assemble bag

3. Stack front layers of bag, with blue circle on bottom, right side down. Add a batting circle. Place white circle on top, with web pattern face up. Match points for top of bag, and baste layers together.

To stitch spider web, use yellow crochet thread in bobbin (wind by hand) and regular thread on top. With web design up, machine-stitch straight lines; begin at one edge of circle and go straight across. Then stitch the inner curved lines. Pull thread ends to back and tie to secure.

To flatten edge, machine-stitch around circle with blue thread; use a zigzag stitch if your machine has one. Lightly press edge. Trim batting and white fabric along edge.

4. Stack back layers, placing blue circle right side up, over batting. Pin to hold. With blue side up, stitch around edge, press and trim.

5. To prepare boxing, begin with the two short lengths. On each strip, turn one long (12½") edge ¼" to the wrong side and press. Place a short strip of fusible interfacing on the wrong side of each strip; cover the wide portion (not the ¼" turn). Press to bond.

Place remaining strip of fusible interfacing on wrong side of long blue strip, and press to bond.

6. To add zipper, use short boxing strips. Open folded edge

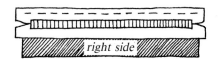

Fig. 1 *Adding zipper*

of one strip and place along the zipper edge, right sides together. Center zipper (Fig. 1). Use a zipper foot and stitch a ¼" seam. To avoid stitching past the zipper pull, open zipper halfway. Stitch until you reach zipper pull, leave needle in fabric, lift presser foot and carefully slide the pull past needle. Continue stitching.

Repeat step to stitch free edge of zipper to other short boxing strip. Trim tape ends.

From right side, finger-press seams along zipper. Then cover with cloth and press with iron. Hand-sew inner edges of tape together at top end of zipper (above pull).

7. Add batting to wrong side of boxing. On each side of zipper section, place a 12½" strip of batting, slipping batting under zipper tape. Catch batting to tape by hand. Machine-stitch each 12½" side, ¼" from raw edge of fabric, catching batting to boxing.

Place long strip of batting against wrong side of long boxing strip and machine-stitch each 18½" side, ¼" from edge.

Trim batting close to the stitching on each section. Then slash seam allowances along stitching at ½" intervals. (This will let boxing fabric spread when stitched to front and back circles.)

8. Prepare shoulder straps. Use the 44"-long cord to tie a knot at the center of the 42"-long cord. Trim ends to make them even.

9. Position cord ends on zipper boxing section (Fig. 2). Place two cords at each end of boxing (on right side), letting cut ends of cord extend ¼"

beyond boxing. Keep cords inside stitching along edges (to avoid catching cord later when boxing is stitched to front and back circles). Sew cord to seam allowances by hand.

Pin long boxing strip to zipper strip, right sides together, to make a ring. Stitch ¼" seams, catching cords in place. Trim batting close to stitching. Press seam allowances away from zipper section.

10. Pin boxing ring to front of bag with center of zipper at top of bag. Stitch, following stitched lines on boxing.

Open zipper halfway. Pin and stitch boxing to back of bag. Turn bag to right side and press lightly.

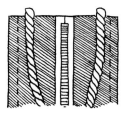

Fig. 2 *Adding cords*

11. To make lining, work first with short boxing strips. Press one long (12½") edge of each strip ¼" to wrong side. Then pin both short strips to long boxing strip, right sides together; match outside raw edges and keep folded edges at center. (There will be a ½" opening at center.) Stitch seams and press seam allowances against long strip.

Stitch boxing to circles. Slip lining into bag. Pin in place and hand-stitch to zipper.

Make spider

12. Trace spider pattern on two layers of yellow felt and cut out. On top layer, mark and embroider face. Use blue floss, with a stem stitch for mouth and a satin stitch for eyes.

13. Stitch felt layers together, using yellow floss and a blanket stitch; stuff with fiberfill before closing.

14. Use the four 4" lengths of chenille stems to make the legs. (Each length will form a pair of legs.) First bend all ends back ¼" to eliminate sharp points.

Position legs on back of spider body, so legs are centered and run horizontally across body. Hand-stitch to body.

To shape legs, bend to make a center joint in each leg. Bend two pairs of legs forward and two pairs backward (see photo).

15. Position spider on lower right of bag and attach with hidden stitches. Catch body and the end of each leg to bag.

MULTICOLOR SHOULDER BAG

(color photo, page 49)

Mix four fabrics to make this 7½x10½" bag that's pieced and quilted at the same time.

You can combine solid colors or prints. If you choose solid colors, use medium-weight fabrics.

There are no patterns needed for the bag, but you may want to make a template for marking the strips.

MATERIALS
8 strips of fabric, 2½x12" each (2 strips each of red, royal blue, yellow, and aqua or green)

Royal blue print, 10¾x15¼", for lining
Muslin (or other lightweight fabric), 12x16½", for backing
Firm interfacing (not fusible), 10¾x14¾"
Thin polyester batting, 12x16½"
9" royal blue zipper
45" narrow royal blue cord, for shoulder strap
Blue thread

DIRECTIONS
For extra help with templates and stitching, see *Sewing Guides,* page 1.

Cut fabric
1. To cut sizes needed for each fabric, follow list of materials.

To measure fabric strips, you can make a template, 2½x12". Trace template on wrong side of fabric and cut out on pencil lines.

Seam allowances are included in all measurements.

Assemble bag
2. Stack layers for stitching. Lay muslin backing flat. Next, add batting and pin edges together. (One 12" side will be top edge of bag.)

For top layer, place first strip (red), right side up; keep one long edge along top edges of batting and muslin. Pin long edges of strip to other layers, but do not stitch.

3. Place second strip (blue) on top of first strip, right sides together and raw edges even. Pin lower edges through all layers (Fig. 3); keep muslin backing smooth.

Machine-stitch pinned seam, ¼" from edges; hold layers taut to keep them from shifting. Turn blue strip to right side and press.

4. Add third strip (yellow), placing it on top of blue strip, right sides together and raw edges matching. Pin, stitch, turn and press.

5. Add fourth strip (aqua or green) in same manner.

Keep adding strips in the same color order.

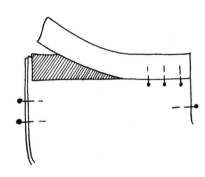

Fig. 3 *Piecing strips*

6. When last strip is turned and pressed, pin long raw edge to batting and muslin (trim batting and muslin if necessary). Machine-baste, ¼" from bottom edge. (Lengthen stitch and loosen tension for basting.) Carefully trim batting and muslin close to stitching.

Repeat step at top edge, stitching the first strip and trimming batting and muslin in same manner.

7. Place zipper against top edge of bag, right sides together, with zipper centered. Baste by hand.

Use zipper foot to stitch ¼" from edge, beginning and ending just past zipper; leave tape ends free. To avoid stitching past the zipper pull (to keep seam straight), open zipper part way. Stitch until you reach pull, leave needle in fabric, lift presser foot and slide pull past needle. Finish stitching seam.

Pin and stitch free edge of zipper to bottom strip of bag (this joins the top and bottom strips).

8. To close seam at each end of zipper, pin fabric edges together, matching basting lines. Begin at each outside edge and stitch a ¼" seam, ending as close to zipper as you can. Press seam open.

Check seam from right side. If there is a gap at either end, close it with a few slip stitches.

9. To close bag sides, keep bag wrong side out, with zipper at top and opened halfway. Pin edges on one side together, matching seam lines on pieced strips. Inside (against right side of fabric), center cord over middle seam lines; have cut end of cord even with fabric edges. By hand, sew cord to seam allowance.

Stitch side with a ½" seam, catching cord. Trim seam ends.

Repeat step to close other side of bag, inserting free end of cord before stitching.

10. Turn bag to right side. Run cord along side seam to top edge of bag and pin. Sew in place with hidden stitches.

Add lining

11. Center interfacing on wrong side of lining (¼" of lining extends beyond interfacing at top and bottom). Stitch interfacing to lining at top and bottom.

12. Fold lining in half, right side inside. Stitch sides together with ¼" seams. Trim interfacing close to stitching. Trim fabric across corners at seam ends.

Fold top edges of lining ¼" to wrong side (over interfacing) and press.

13. Slip lining into bag and hand-stitch folded edge of lining to zipper tape.

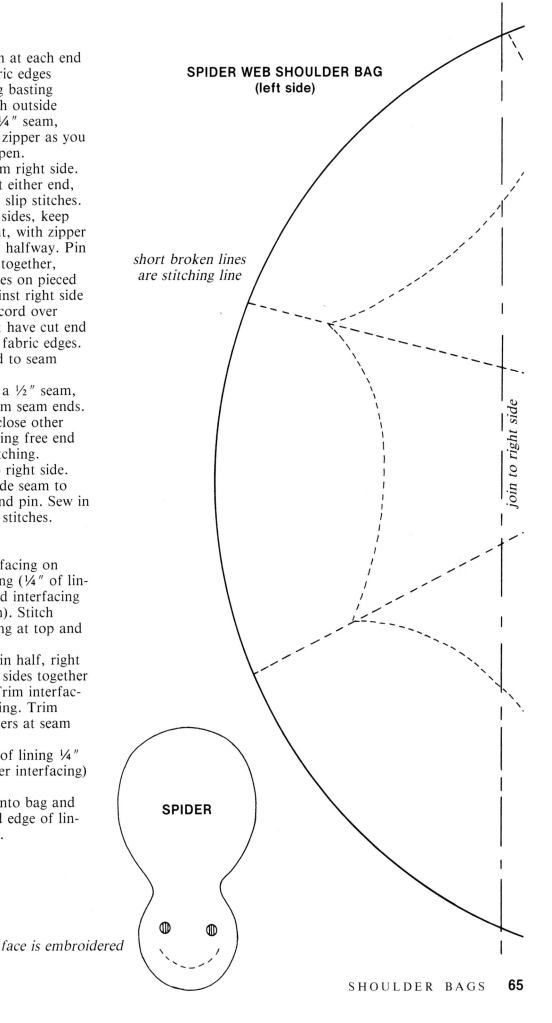

SPIDER WEB SHOULDER BAG
(left side)

short broken lines are stitching line

join to right side

SPIDER

face is embroidered

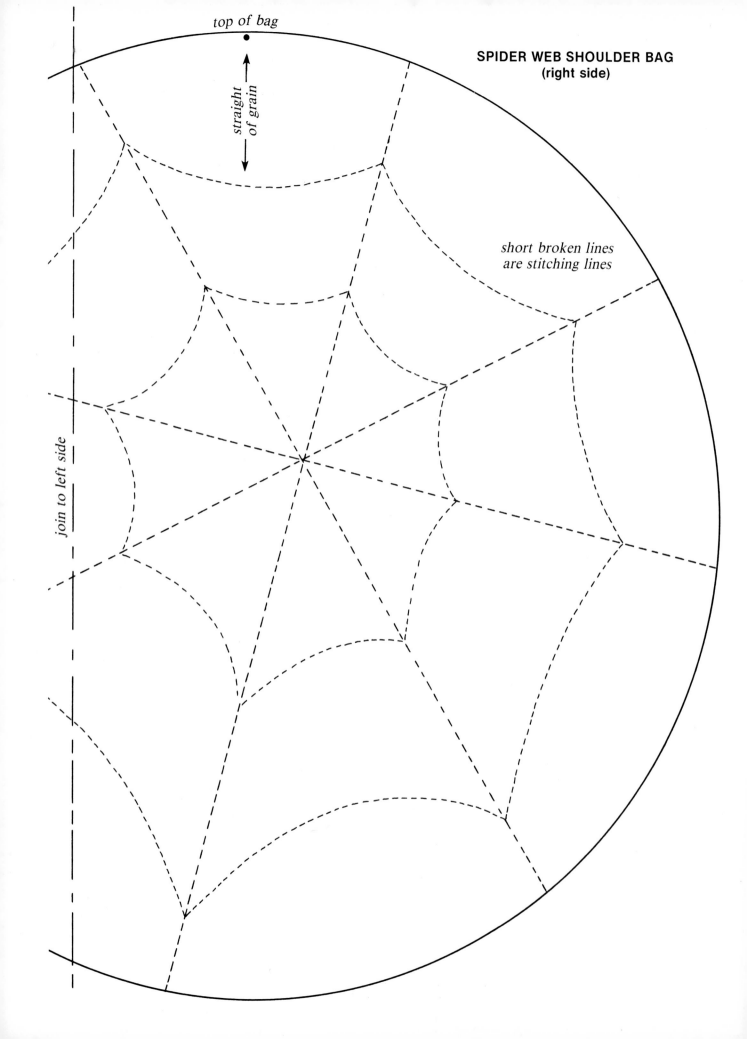

top of bag

straight
of grain

SPIDER WEB SHOULDER BAG
(right side)

short broken lines
are stitching lines

join to left side

Little Accent Pillows

Only 10" across, these little flower and leaf pillows add bright spots to a group of plain pillows. One is just the right size to tuck in the corner of a chair without crowding the "sitting" space.

Flower petals and leaves are padded and stitched, then attached to the pillow front. The outside pillow cover is removable, with a zipper across the back. An inner pillow of muslin slips inside.

GENERAL DIRECTIONS
Follow directions for each pillow, referring to general guides below as needed.

To make pillow back
Pin the two half circles along the straight edges, right sides together; match pencil lines. At each end, machine-stitch from outside edge to ½" inside the pencil line circle.

Machine-baste center section of seam. (Lengthen stitch and loosen tension for basting.) Press seam open.

On wrong side, center zipper over seam, face down. (Edges of zipper will run along edges of seam allowances.) Pin zipper in place. Keep fabric flat and use zipper foot to stitch zipper to fabric, ¼" from zipper edge (Fig. 1). Remove machine basting at center of seam.

To join pillow front to back
On pillow back, open zipper halfway. On pillow front, fold petals or leaves away from outside seam line and pin.

Place pillow front against back, right sides together; match straight grain lines. Pin and baste layers together, matching pencil lines along circles. Machine-stitch. Finish seams by stitching a zigzag or straight line along edges.

Turn pillow cover to right side and press lightly.

To make inner pillow
Pin muslin circles together. Machine-stitch on pencil line, leaving 4" open for turning. Turn to right side and press. Stuff pillow to medium firmness with fiberfill, keeping shape flat. Close opening by hand.

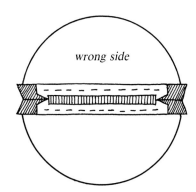

Fig. 1 *Adding zipper*

DAISY

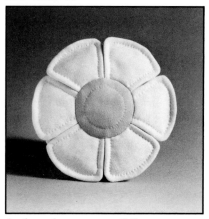

(color photo, page 84)

Six separate petals and a center form the flower. Use a firm, medium-weight fabric for the pillow cover and petals.

MATERIALS
½ yd. off-white fabric, 44" wide, for pillow cover and petals
Yellow fabric, 5" square, for flower center
Muslin or other white fabric, 12x29", for inner pillow and backing for flower center
Thread to match fabrics
Thin polyester batting, 9x20"
Polyester fiberfill
9" white zipper

DIRECTIONS
For extra help with patterns, templates and stitching, see *Sewing Guides*, page 1.

Cut patterns and fabric

1. Trace pattern pieces for Daisy, page 72. Trace half circle, page 71, and make a full circle pattern for pillow front; copy inner circle No. 1. Also trace a half-circle pattern for the back.

Cut out patterns, and make a template for the petal. Seam allowances will be added when cutting fabric.

2. On wrong side of off-white fabric, place front and back patterns, leaving space for ½″ seam allowances. Trace one front and mark inner circle. Trace two back pieces, and mark ½″ seam allowances along the straight edges (to make them exact). Cut out pieces, adding ½″ seam allowances.

Fold remaining off-white fabric to make two layers, right side inside. On top, trace six petals, leaving space for ¼″ seam allowances. Cut out around outside curves, adding ¼″ seam allowances. On each top curve, cut on pencil lines. Pin each petal unit over batting and cut batting around shape.

On right side of yellow fabric, trace flower center; mark quilting line. Cut out, adding ¼″ seam allowance.

On muslin and on batting, trace one flower center and cut out just inside pencil lines.

On two layers of muslin, trace front pattern (full circle). Cut out, adding ¼″ seam allowances.

Make flower

3. To form each petal, keep layers right sides together, with batting on the bottom. Stitch around outside curve on pencil line, leaving top curve open.

Trim batting to stitching line. Trim seam allowance along the stitching to just under ¼″. Turn petal to right side and press lightly.

By hand or machine, use matching thread and quilt around each petal, ³⁄₈″ from edge.

4. Make flower center. Use yellow thread and stitch over outside circle (pencil line) to mark turning line. Place batting on wrong side, inside stitching. Add white muslin circle and baste layers together.

By hand or machine, use matching thread and quilt the inside circle.

Turn raw edge of flower center to wrong side (over muslin and batting) and baste; trim batting where necessary.

Assemble pillow

5. On wrong side of pillow front, use matching thread to machine-stitch over pencil lines on outside seam and inner circle. (This transfers lines to the right side.) Press flat.

6. Position petals on right side of pillow front, matching top curve of petals to inner circle on front. Edges of petals will butt together; outside curve of each petal will extend beyond seam line on pillow front. Baste petals in place.

Machine-stitch around inside curve of petals (inner circle), ³⁄₁₆″ from edge. Use a zigzag if your machine has one, keeping within the ³⁄₁₆″ seam allowance.

7. Position flower center over petals, covering stitching line on petals, and pin. Sew in place by hand, tucking in a little fiberfill before closing.

8. To make pillow back and to join pillow front to back, follow *General Directions*.

9. Unpin petals and smooth out. Pin center of each petal to pillow front, ½″ from outside edge. Attach with hidden stitches.

10. To make inner pillow, follow *General Directions*. Slip inner pillow into Daisy cover and close zipper.

ORANGE FLOWER

(color photo, page 84)

Each layer of petals is stitched as a unit, then attached to the pillow front. Choose a firm, medium-weight fabric that doesn't ravel.

MATERIALS

¾ yd. orange fabric, 44″ wide, for pillow cover and petals
Yellow fabric, 4″ square, for flower center
Muslin or other white fabric, 12x24″, for inner pillow
Thread to match fabrics
Thin polyester batting, 12x20″
Polyester fiberfill
9″ orange zipper

DIRECTIONS

For extra help with patterns, templates and stitching, see *Sewing Guides*, page 1.

Cut patterns and fabric

1. Trace half patterns for large petals, page 73, and for small petals, page 74, and make full patterns. Trace flower center, page 74. Trace half circle, page 71, and make a full circle pattern for pillow front; copy inner circles No. 1 and No. 2. Also trace a half-circle pattern for the back.

Cut out patterns, and make a template for flower center. Seam allowances will be added when cutting fabric.

2. On wrong side of orange fabric, place front and back patterns, leaving space for ½" seam allowances. Trace one front; mark inner circles. Trace two back pieces, marking ½" seam allowances along the straight edges (to make them exact). Cut out pieces, adding ½" seam allowances.

Fold remaining orange fabric to make two layers, right side inside. On top, trace patterns for large petals and small petals, leaving room for ¼" seam allowances. Cut out around outside edges, adding ¼" seam allowances; cut out center circles on pencil lines.

Pin layers of each petal unit over batting and cut out around shape.

On right side of yellow, trace flower center. Cut out, adding ¼" seam allowance.

On batting, trace flower center and cut out just inside pencil line.

On two layers of muslin, trace front pattern (full circle). Cut out, adding ¼" seam allowances.

Make flower

3. To form each layer of petals, keep fabric right sides together, with batting on the bottom. Stitch around outside edge on pencil line; at each V point, take one stitch across point.

Trim batting to stitching line. Trim fabric seam allowance along the stitching to just under ¼". Turn fabric to right side and press lightly.

Place paper pattern on right side of each petal layer and mark stitching lines to divide petals. With orange thread, machine-stitch lines. *Note:* To hide thread ends at the outside edge, tie a knot and put ends through a needle. Insert needle at end of the stitching, work needle through batting and bring it up on back of petals. Clip threads close to fabric.

By hand or machine, use matching thread and quilt from center circle around each petal shape, ⅜" from edge (Fig. 2).

4. Make flower center. Use yellow thread and stitch over pencil line to mark turning line.

Place batting circle on wrong side, inside stitching. Turn raw edge of flower center to wrong side (over batting) and baste; trim batting where necessary.

Fig. 2 *Quilting petal shapes*

Assemble pillow

5. On wrong side of pillow front, use matching thread to machine-stitch over pencil lines on outside seam and inner circles. (This transfers lines to the right side.) Press flat.

6. Position large petal layer on right side of front, matching top curve of petals to inner circle No. 1. Outside curves of petals will extend beyond outside seam on front circle. Baste in place.

Machine-stitch around inside curve of petals, ³⁄₁₆" from edge. Use a zigzag if your machine has one, keeping within the ³⁄₁₆" seam allowance.

Add small petal layer, matching center circle on petals with inner circle No. 2 on pillow front. Each small petal should be centered on a large petal. Baste and stitch around inside curve of petals, as for large petal layer.

7. Position flower center over petals, covering stitching on petals, and pin. Sew in place by hand, tucking in a little fiberfill before closing.

8. To make pillow back and to join pillow front to back, follow *General Directions.*

9. Unpin petals and smooth out. Pin center of each petal to background fabric, ½" from outside edge. Attach with hidden stitches.

Pin center of each petal in top layer to bottom petal layer, ½" from edge. Attach with hidden stitches.

10. To make inner pillow, follow *General Directions.* Slip inner pillow into Orange Flower cover and close zipper.

GREEN VINE

(color photo, page 84)

The design is formed by eighteen leaves, each padded and stitched separately.

Choose a firm, medium-weight yellow fabric for the pillow front and back. Use a lightweight green fabric for the leaves.

MATERIALS

Yellow fabric, 12x24", for pillow front and back
3/8 yd. green fabric, 44" wide, for leaves
Muslin or other white fabric, 12x24", for inner pillow
Thread to match fabrics
Thin polyester batting, 13x23"
Polyester fiberfill
9" yellow zipper

DIRECTIONS

For extra help with patterns, templates and stitching, see *Sewing Guides,* page 1.

Cut patterns and fabric

1. Trace leaf patterns, page 74. Trace half-circle pattern, page 71, and make a full circle pattern for pillow front; mark center of circle. Also trace a half-circle pattern for the back.

Cut out patterns, and make templates for the leaves. Seam allowances will be added when cutting fabric.

2. On wrong side of yellow fabric, place front and back patterns, leaving space for ½" seam allowances. Trace one front and mark center. Trace two back pieces, marking ½" seam allowances along the straight edges (to make them exact). Cut out pieces, adding ½" seam allowances.

Fold green fabric in half along the lengthwise grain to make two layers, right side inside. On top, trace six large leaves and twelve small leaves, leaving 1" between them. Cut out rectangles around leaves ½" beyond pencil lines. Pin green rectangles over batting and cut out around shape.

On two layers of muslin, trace front pattern (full circle). Cut out, adding ¼" seam allowances.

Make leaves

3. Keep layers for each leaf pinned together, with batting on the bottom. Machine-stitch on pencil line around curve; leave open between dots.

Trim batting close to the stitching line. Cut around curve, leaving seam allowance under ¼"; trim seam allowance at point.

Turn each leaf to right side. Close opening with slip stitches and press lightly.

By hand or machine, quilt a center line on each leaf.

Assemble pillow

4. On wrong side of pillow front, use matching thread to machine-stitch over pencil seam line. (This transfers line to right side.) Press flat.

5. On right side of pillow front, position large leaves around center; let each leaf overlap an adjoining leaf (see photo). Pin in place.

Use two small leaves to form a vine from each large leaf. Outside leaf should overlap seam line on pillow front about 3/16".

With hidden stitches, attach top of each large leaf to pillow front and to adjoining leaf. Attach top of each small leaf to pillow front in the same way.

Attach free end of each large leaf to pillow front, ¼" from tip. Attach free end of middle group of leaves in the same way. Leave tips of outside leaves free until pillow front is stitched to back.

6. To make pillow back and to join pillow front to back, follow *General Directions.*

7. Unpin leaves and smooth out. Catch free ends of outside leaves to pillow front, ½" from the tips.

8. To make inner pillow, follow *General Directions.* Slip inner pillow into Green Vine cover and close zipper.

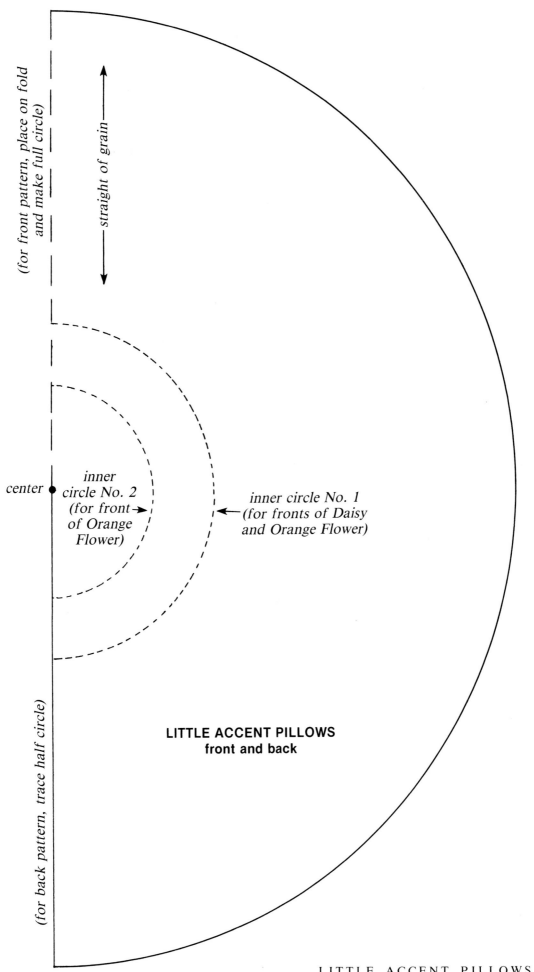

(for front pattern, place on fold and make full circle)

← *straight of grain* →

center •

inner circle No. 2 (for front of Orange Flower)

inner circle No. 1 (for fronts of Daisy and Orange Flower) ←

LITTLE ACCENT PILLOWS
front and back

(for back pattern, trace half circle)

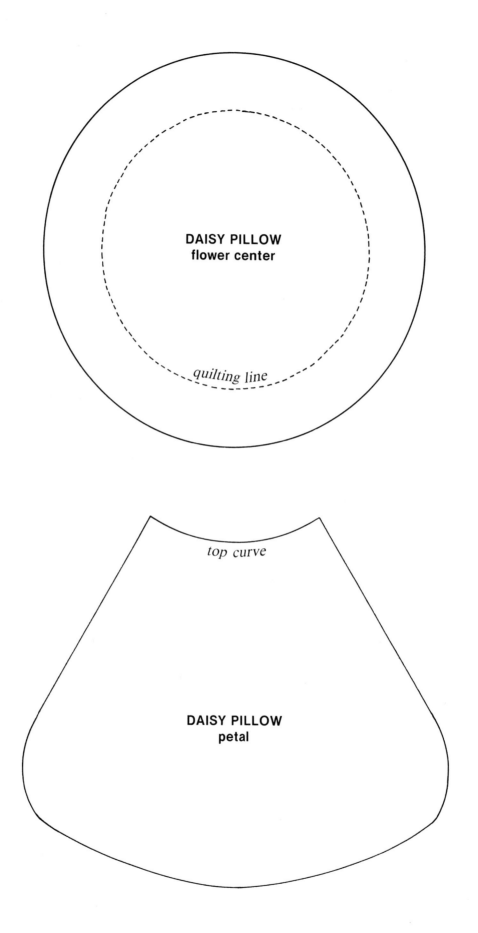

DAISY PILLOW
flower center

quilting line

top curve

DAISY PILLOW
petal

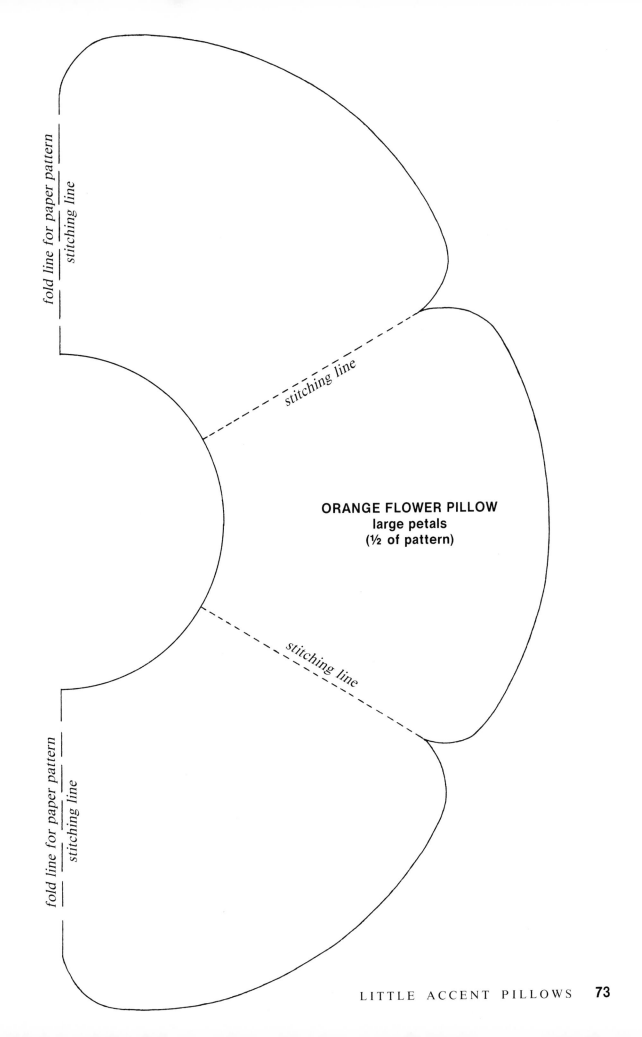

fold line for paper pattern

stitching line

stitching line

ORANGE FLOWER PILLOW
large petals
(½ of pattern)

stitching line

fold line for paper pattern

stitching line

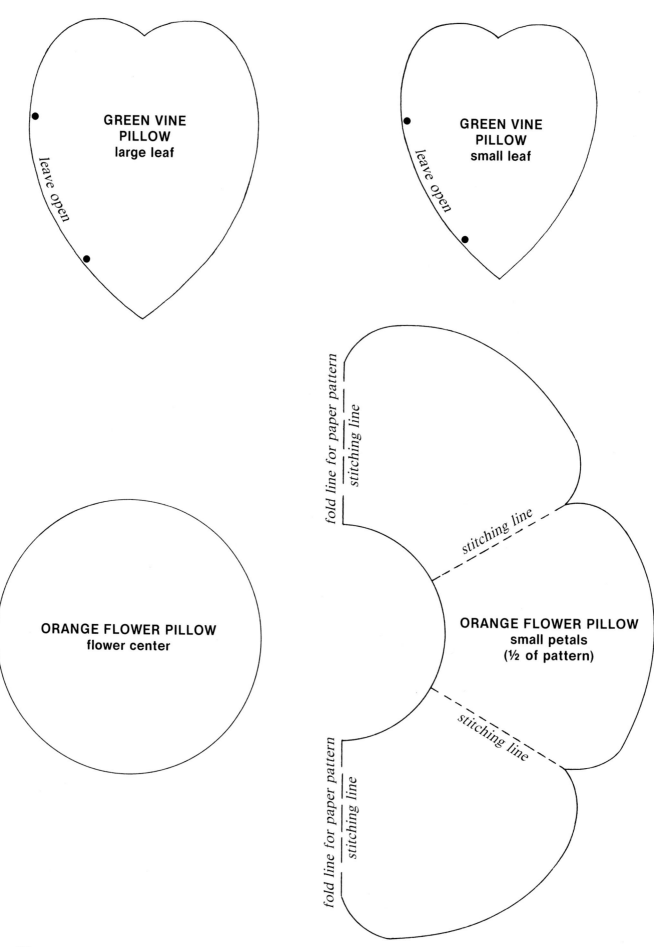

GREEN VINE PILLOW
large leaf

leave open

GREEN VINE PILLOW
small leaf

leave open

fold line for paper pattern
stitching line

stitching line

ORANGE FLOWER PILLOW
flower center

ORANGE FLOWER PILLOW
small petals
(½ of pattern)

stitching line

fold line for paper pattern
stitching line

Funny Face Pillows (or Pajama Bags)

The Pigtail Doll and the Puppy are perfect for a child's room. Each 15"-circle pillow cover has a zipper closing down the back. You can make an inner pillow to fill it, or leave it empty to be stuffed with a pair of pajamas.

Each pillow front is stacked over a layer of batting and a layer of muslin (backing). These are held together with a few lines of machine stitching (quilting). The pillow back also has a layer of muslin backing to add firmness.

Choose firm fabrics that don't ravel easily. For the large pieces, you could use a medium-weight sportswear fabric.

GENERAL DIRECTIONS
Follow directions for each pillow, referring to general guides below as needed.

To make pillow back
Lay one back piece (half circle) flat, right side down. On top, place muslin backing, with pencil lines up. Pin layers together, matching pencil lines.

Repeat to pin muslin backing to other back piece. Then handle each double layer as one piece.

To join back pieces, position the two half circles, right sides together. Match pencil lines along straight edges and pin.

Machine-stitch each end of seam line; begin at outside edge and stitch to 1½" inside pencil line on circle.

Machine-baste center section of seam. (Lengthen stitch and loosen tension for basting.) Press seam open. Trim seam allowance on muslin close to stitching.

On wrong side, center zipper over seam, face down. (Edges of zipper will run along edges of seam allowances.) Pin zipper in place. Keep fabric flat and use zipper foot to stitch zipper to fabric, ¼" from zipper edge. Stitch a continuous seam, taking a few stitches across zipper tape at each end (Fig. 1). Remove machine basting at center of seam. By hand, overcast edge of zipper tape to raw edge of fabric.

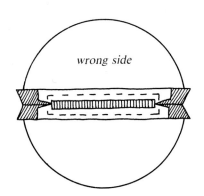

Fig. 1 *Adding zipper*

Pin muslin to backing along outside circle. Use thread in machine to match back fabric. With muslin side up, machine-baste around outside circle over pencil line.

To join pillow front to back
On pillow back, open zipper halfway. Place pillow front against back, right sides together, with zipper seam meeting top and bottom dots on front layer. Match stitched lines along circles, pin and baste.

Use thread to match back fabric. With front layer up, machine-stitch around circle. Add a second stitching; use a zigzag close to first line or a straight stitch ⅛" away. Trim seam to ¼" (do not cut stitching).

Turn cover to right side, work seam to edge and press lightly.

To make inner pillow
Pin muslin circles together. Machine-stitch on pencil line, leaving 4" open for turning. Turn to right side and press. Stuff inner pillow firmly with fiberfill, keeping shape flat. Close opening by hand.

PIGTAIL DOLL

(color photo, page 83)

The pigtails are made of bulky rug yarn that matches the fabric hair appliqué. Use red, as shown, or choose another color.

Rug yarn comes in a hank, with rings about 50″ around, so it's easy to cut in half for braiding. If you can't find the right color, you could buy a pull-out skein of bulky yarn and wind it into a hank.

MATERIALS

½ yd. red firm fabric, 44″ wide, for hair appliqué and pillow back
White firm fabric, 17″ square, for pillow front
Bright blue fabric scrap, for eyes
Bright pink fabric scrap, for cheeks
Blue fabric with stripe or print, 13½″ square, for hair ties
½ yd. muslin (or other light-weight fabric), 44″ wide, for backing pillow front and back
½ yd. muslin, for inner pillow
Thread to match fabrics
Black embroidery floss
1 hank red rug yarn (about 1.35 oz.)
Thin polyester batting, 17″ square, for pillow front
Polyester fiberfill, for inner pillow
12″ red zipper

DIRECTIONS

For extra help with patterns, stitching, appliqué and stuffing, see *Sewing Guides,* page 1.

Cut patterns and fabric

1. Trace half pattern for face, pages 79-80, joining sections on broken lines; copy all design lines and division dots on circle. Make a full pattern, and go over inside lines with a pen to make them darker.

From full pattern, trace a separate pattern for hair and cut out. Trace patterns for eye and cheek, and make templates. Seam allowances will be added when cutting fabric.

2. On right side of white fabric, pin full circle face pattern; have arrow on straight grain of fabric. Trace outside circle only; mark quarter division dots just outside circle. Cut out, adding ½″ seam allowance.

Place white fabric circle over face pattern, matching circle lines and dots. Tape layers together. Very lightly, trace lines for appliqués, embroidery and quilting.

On right side of red fabric, trace hair appliqué; copy lines for quilting. (Be sure to leave enough fabric for pillow back pieces.) Cut out hair, adding ½″ seam allowance to outside edge and ¼″ seam allowance to inside hair lines.

Fold face pattern in half to make a half-circle pattern for back. On wrong side of red fabric, trace two half circles, leaving room for ½″ seam allowances. On straight edges, mark ½″ seam allowances (to make them exact). Cut out fabric, adding ½″ seam allowances.

On right side of blue fabric, trace two eyes. On right side of pink, trace two cheeks. Cut out, adding ¼″ seam allowances.

On wrong side of blue fabric with stripe, mark two rectangles for hair ties, 6½x13½″ each. Cut out on pencil lines.

On single layer of muslin, trace full circle pattern and two half circles (for backing pillow front and back). Cut out, adding ½″ seam allowances. On two layers of muslin, trace full circle pattern (for inner pillow). Cut out, adding ¼″ seam allowances.

On batting, place full circle pattern and cut out around shape, adding ½″ seam allowance.

Assemble pillow cover

3. Prepare appliqués for hair, eyes and cheeks. With matching thread, stay-stitch V points on hair and cheeks, and slash to stitching at V points.

Turn seam allowances on appliqués to wrong side. Baste and press. *Note:* Do not turn seam allowance on outside edge of hair. It will be caught in the seam allowance when pillow front is stitched to the back.

4. Position hair appliqué on white face circle, following pencil guide lines; match lines on outside circles. Pin and baste hair in place. Attach turned edges with matching thread and a hemming stitch.

Position eyes and cheeks, and baste in place. Attach with matching thread and a hemming stitch. Before closing cheeks, tuck in a little fiberfill.

5. Embroider eye circles, using two strands of black floss and a blanket stitch. Embroider mouth, nose tip and eyebrows, using two strands of black floss and a chain stitch.

6. Stack fabric layers. Lay muslin circle flat. Add batting circle. On top, place appliquéd face layer, right side up. Pin and baste layers together.

7. Add quilting lines. With white thread, machine-stitch on face; follow edge of hair appliqué, keeping close to appliqué.

Quilt nose line. Begin at one eyebrow and stitch down side of nose. Continue under embroidered nose tip (close to embroidery), and go up other side of nose to meet eyebrow.

Also stitch a line under embroidered mouth, close to embroidery.

With red thread, stitch lines on hair, from inside edge to top of circle.

8. With matching thread and a long stitch, machine-stitch around outside circle (change thread to match fabric).

9. To make pillow back and to join pillow front to back, follow *General Directions*.

10. To make hair ties, fold each blue stripe rectangle in half, right side inside, along the 13½″ length. Pin edges together and stitch a ¼″ seam across one end and along the 13½″ length. Turn to right side, work seams to edge and press. Turn raw edges ¼″ to the inside and close seam with slip stitches. Press.

11. To make braids, open hank of yarn to form a large ring. From one cut end, cut off four lengths, 6″ each.

Tie a 6″ length of yarn around the strands at each end of ring, dividing ring into two equal parts. With ties at each end, cut across yarns to divide ring in half.

On each half, divide the strands into three units. Slip a fabric hair tie under one unit and tie a single knot, covering yarn tie. Make a loose braid of yarn. Tie end of braid with a 6″ length of yarn. Trim yarn ends.

12. Position braids on pillow cover and sew fabric ties to cover.

This completes the cover for a pajama bag.

Add inner pillow

13. To use the cover as a pillow, make an inner pillow, following *General Directions*. Slip inner pillow into cover and close zipper. *Note:* Edge of pillow will not be crisp. You can add fiberfill (between cover and inner pillow) to help smooth out the edge, if you wish.

PUPPY

(color photo, page 83)

The white muzzle, with embroidered mouth line, is padded with a layer of batting. The red tongue is stitched separately and added last.

MATERIALS
½ yd. medium brown firm fabric, 44″ wide, for face appliqués and pillow back
White firm fabric, 17x29″, for pillow front and muzzle appliqué
Black fabric, 11x12″, for ears, eyes and nose
Red lightweight fabric, 5x8″, for tongue
½ yd. muslin (or other lightweight fabric), 44″ wide, for backing pillow front and back
½ yd. muslin, for inner pillow
Thread to match fabrics
Black embroidery floss
Thin polyester batting, 17x33″
Polyester fiberfill, for inner pillow
12″ medium brown zipper

DIRECTIONS
For extra help with patterns, stitching, appliqué and stuffing, see *Sewing Guides*, page 1.

Cut patterns and fabric

1. Trace half pattern for face, pages 81-82, joining sections on broken lines; copy all design lines and division dots on circle. Make a full pattern, and go over inside lines with a pen to make them darker.

From full pattern, trace a separate pattern for face side, brow and muzzle. Trace pattern for ear, page 81. Also trace patterns for eye, nose and tongue, and make templates.

Cut out patterns and templates. Seam allowances will be added when cutting fabric.

2. On right side of white fabric, pin full circle face pattern; have arrow on straight grain of fabric. Trace outside circle only; mark division dots just outside circle. Cut out, adding ½" seam allowance.

Place white fabric circle over face pattern, matching circle lines and dots. Tape layers together. Very lightly, trace lines for face side, brow and eye appliqués.

On right side of white fabric, trace muzzle; copy lines for embroidery and for placing nose appliqué. Cut out, adding ½" seam allowance to outside edge (bottom curve), and ¼" seam allowance to upper curve.

On right side of medium brown fabric, trace two face sides (one reversed) and one brow, leaving room for seam allowances. (Be sure to leave enough fabric for the back pieces.) On face sides, copy embroidery lines for eyelids. Cut out side faces, adding ½" seam allowances to outside edges and ¼" seam allowances to inside seam lines. Cut out brow, adding ¼" seam allowances.

Fold face pattern in half to make a half-circle pattern for back. On wrong side of medium brown fabric, trace two half circles, leaving room for ½" seam allowances. On straight edges, mark ½" seam allowances (to make them exact). Cut out fabric, adding ½" seam allowances.

Fold black fabric to make two layers, right side inside. On top, trace two ears and cut out, adding ¼" seam allowances. Using single layer of black, place templates on right side and trace nose and two eyes. Cut out, adding ¼" seam allowances.

Fold red fabric to make two layers, right side inside. On top, trace tongue. Cut out, adding ¼" seam allowance.

On single layer of muslin, trace full circle pattern and two half circles (for backing pillow front and back). Cut out, adding ½" seam allowances. On two layers of muslin, trace full circle pattern (for inner pillow). Cut out, adding ¼" seam allowances.

On batting, trace pattern for muzzle and cut out on pencil line. Trace template for one tongue and two ears; cut out, adding ¼" seam allowances. Place full circle pattern on batting and cut out around shape, adding ½" seam allowance.

Assemble pillow cover

3. Prepare appliqués for face sides, brow, eyes and nose. With matching thread, stay-stitch inside curves on face sides and brow, and V point on nose. Slash to stitching along inside curves and at V point.

Turn seam allowances to wrong side on pencil lines. Baste and press. *Note:* Do not turn seam allowances on outside edges of face sides, or on seams that underlap another appliqué.

For muzzle, place matching batting piece on wrong side of fabric. Fold seam allowance over batting along upper curve and baste; leave bottom curve flat.

4. Position face sides and brow on white face circle, following pencil guide lines; match lines on outside circles. Pin and baste in place.

Lay muzzle on top. Position eyes, with edges under face sides and muzzle. Add nose appliqué. Baste pieces in place.

Attach appliqués with matching thread and a hemming stitch. Begin with bottom layers (eyes and brow).

5. Embroider eyelids and mouth line, using two strands of black floss and a chain stitch.

6. Stack fabric layers. Lay muslin circle flat. Add batting circle. On top, place appliquéd face layer, right side up. Pin and baste layers together.

7. Add quilting lines. With white thread, machine-stitch a line under embroidered mouth (close to embroidery). Also quilt white fabric on forehead; follow along edge of face sides and top of brow, keeping close to appliqués.

With brown thread, stitch face sides, following edge of muzzle; do not stitch on white area under eyes.

8. With matching thread and a long stitch, machine-stitch around outside circle (change thread to match fabric).

9. To make each ear, keep black pieces right sides together, and pin over layer of batting. Stitch over pencil lines on the two long edges; leave bottom edge open. Trim batting close to stitching and trim seam allowance at point. Turn to right side and press.

Pin layers at lower edge of each ear together, and machine-stitch ¼″ from edge. Slash seam allowance to stitching at ¼″ intervals.

10. Position an ear on each side of head, right sides together, with stitched line on ear following line of circle. Pin and baste ear to circle.

11. To make tongue, keep red pieces right sides together, and pin over layer of batting. Stitch on pencil line, leaving opening for turning. Trim batting close to stitching, and trim seam allowance. Turn tongue to right side and press. Close opening with slip stitches. Quilt a line down center of tongue, using red thread and hand or machine stitches.

12. Position tongue inside embroidered mouth line, and attach upper curve of tongue with hidden stitches.

13. To make pillow back and to join pillow front to back, follow *General Directions*.

This completes the Puppy as a pajama bag.

Add inner pillow

14. To use the cover as a pillow, make an inner pillow, following *General Directions*. Slip inner pillow into cover and close zipper. *Note:* Edge of pillow will not be crisp. You can add fiberfill (between cover and inner pillow) to help smooth out the edge, if you wish.

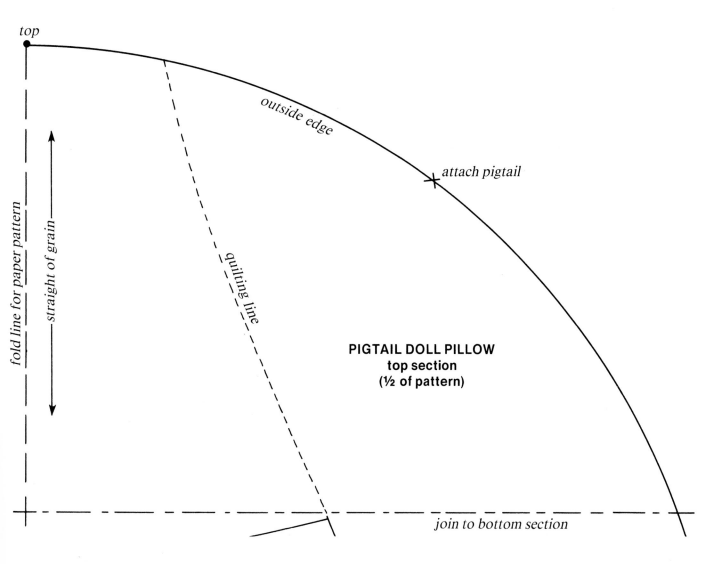

top

outside edge

attach pigtail

fold line for paper pattern

straight of grain

quilting line

PIGTAIL DOLL PILLOW
top section
(½ of pattern)

join to bottom section

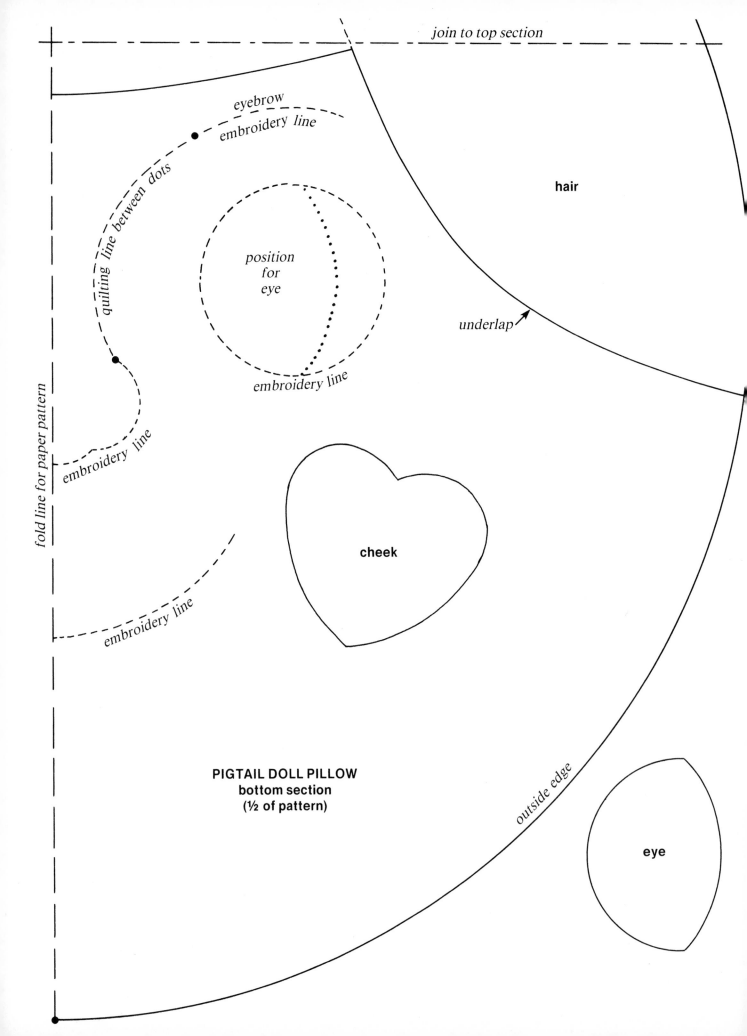

join to top section

eyebrow

embroidery line

quilting line between dots

hair

position for eye

underlap

embroidery line

embroidery line

fold line for paper pattern

cheek

embroidery line

PIGTAIL DOLL PILLOW
bottom section
(½ of pattern)

outside edge

eye

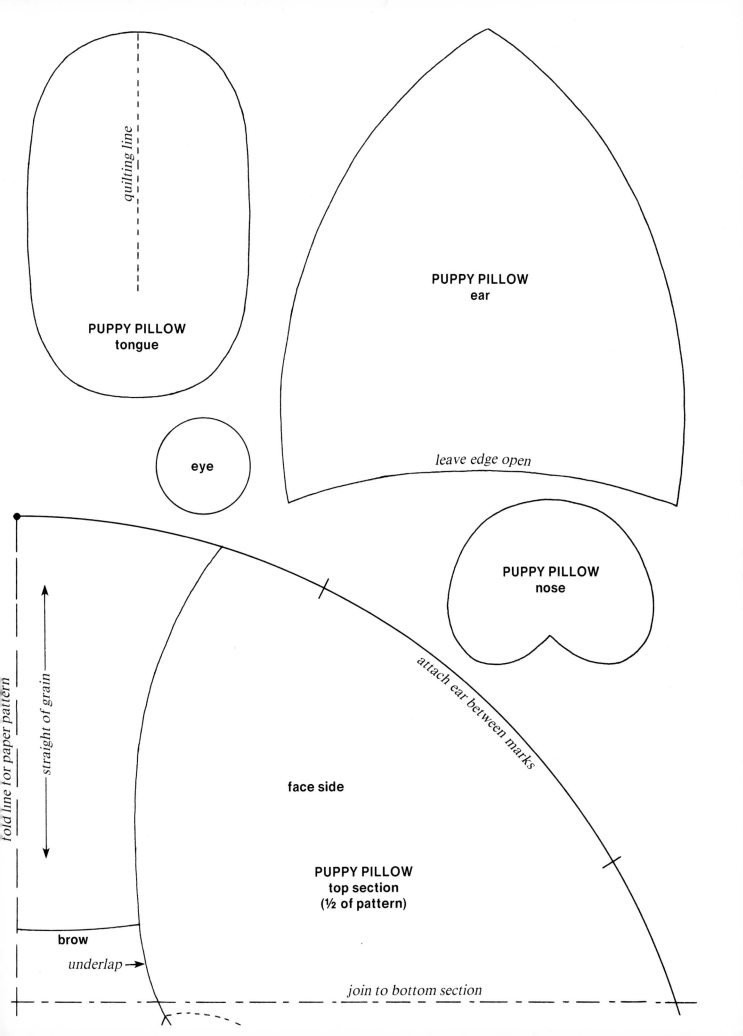

quilting line

PUPPY PILLOW
tongue

PUPPY PILLOW
ear

eye

leave edge open

PUPPY PILLOW
nose

attach ear between marks

face side

fold line for paper pattern

straight of grain

PUPPY PILLOW
top section
(½ of pattern)

brow

underlap →

join to bottom section

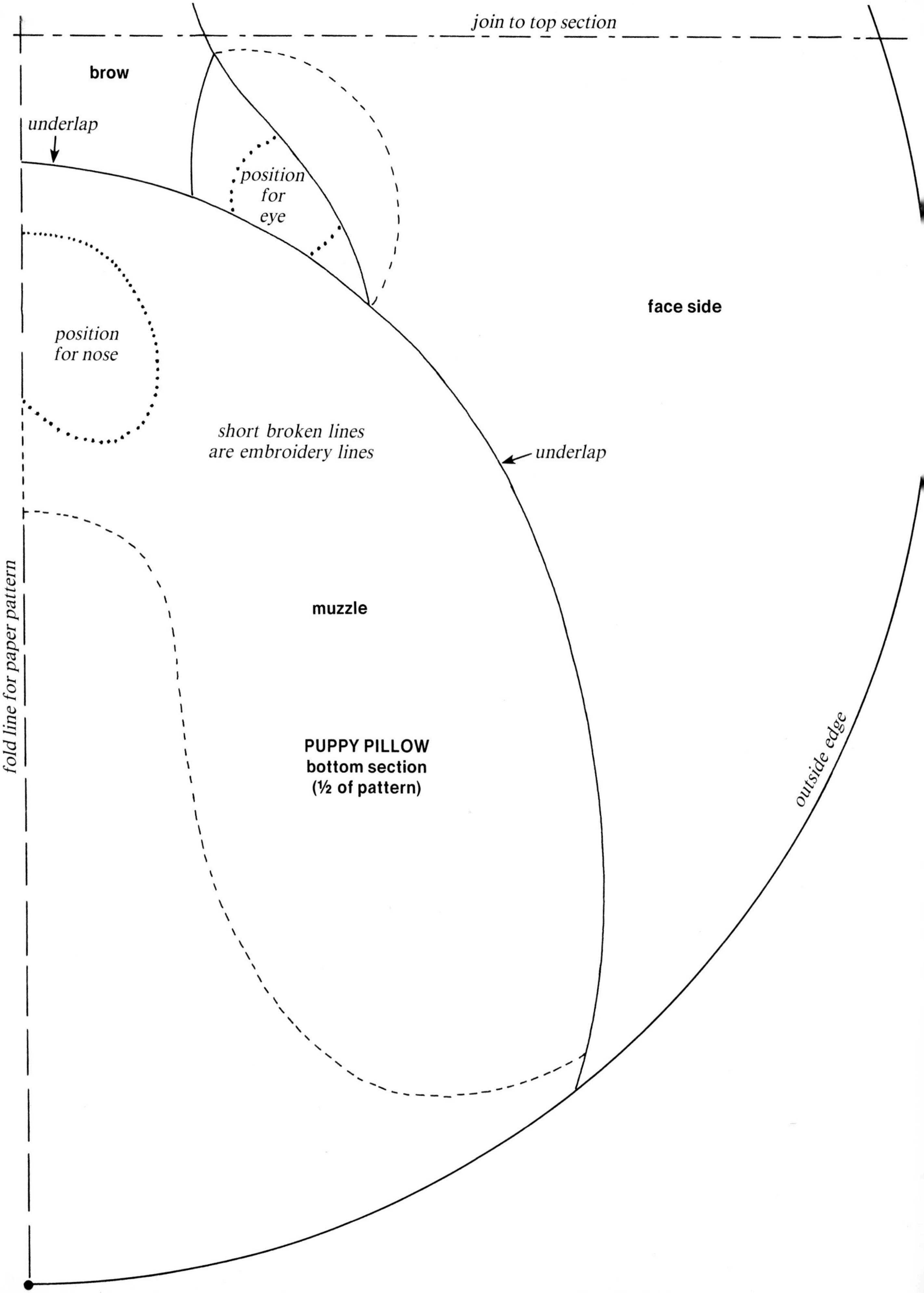

join to top section

brow

underlap

position for eye

face side

position for nose

short broken lines are embroidery lines

underlap

muzzle

fold line for paper pattern

**PUPPY PILLOW
bottom section
(½ of pattern)**

outside edge

Pigtail Doll and Puppy, below, can be used as Funny Face pillows or pajama bags (page 75).

At right are Baby's Dolls (page 10) and Baby's Soft Balls (page l5), easy-to-make toys you can tuck in with other gifts.

83

Mix one of these 10″ Little
Accent Pillows (page 67)
with a pile of plain pillows,
or tuck it into the corner of
a chair. Left to right are
Green Vine, Orange Flower
and Daisy.

84

Fabric Pictures for your wall (page 95) include Surfing Bear, left, and Ruffled Flower, above left.

The felt Fish, above, can be made as Kitchen Magnets (page 9), or you can turn one into a little felt picture (page 10).

The design for the beige pillow at top is Two Triangles. For the rose pillow below, the design is Rail Fence.

Corduroy Patchwork Pillows

Each of these pillows is made from one fabric, even though the patchwork pieces appear to be cut from two fabrics. You take advantage of the way corduroy pile reflects light when you cut and stitch the pieces.

Working with a pile fabric such as corduroy is more challenging than working with a flat fabric. That's because the fabric tends to shift when you are joining the pieces. You need patience—and lots of pins.

The sample pillows are made of corduroy with medium wales (about nine wales to the inch). The finished pillows are 14″ square, and the ruffle trim is optional.

MATERIALS

(for one pillow)
½ yd. corduroy, 44″ wide, for pillow (or ¾ yd. for pillow and ruffle)
2 pieces muslin, 15″ square each, for inner pillow
Thread to match fabric
Buttonhole twist (if ruffle is used) in color to match or blend with corduroy, for gathering
Polyester fiberfill

DIRECTIONS

When you press corduroy, be careful not to flatten the pile. Always press from the wrong side, and cushion the right side by placing it on a special needle pressboard or a thick terry cloth towel.

For extra help with patterns, templates, stitching and stuffing, see *Sewing Guides,* page 1.

Cut pattern and fabric

1. Trace pattern, page 90, and make a template.
For Rail Fence, trace pattern A.

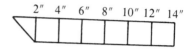

Fig. 1 *Making ruler template*

For Two Triangles, you will need a ruler template 14″ long, marked in 2″ intervals (Fig. 1). Use the 10″ pattern on page 90 as a beginning, and add two more divisions. Mark the 2″ intervals on both sides of the template.

2. Lay fabric flat, wrong side up, with pile running downward.

If you are going to make a ruffle, mark two strips, each 2½″ wide, along one cut edge (across the width).

For the pillow back, mark a 14″ square in one corner; leave at least ¼″ on all sides for seam allowances.

Trace template, following layout for your design. Let straight edges of template follow lines formed by wales, and leave ¼″ on all sides for seam allowances. Mark an arrow on each piece to indicate direction of pile.

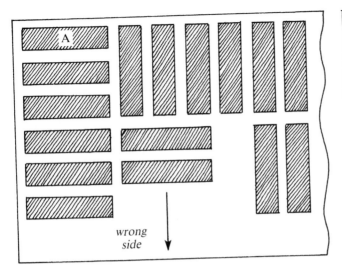

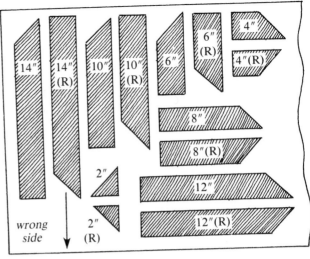

Fig. 2 *Layout for Rail Fence (arrow shows pile direction)*

Fig. 3 *Layout for Two Triangles (arrow shows pile direction)*

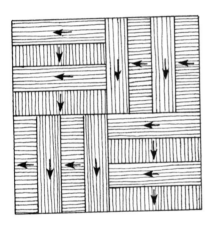

Fig. 4 *Rail Fence (arrows show pile direction)*

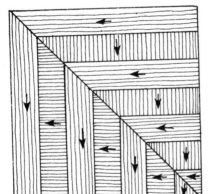

Fig. 5 *Two Triangles (arrows show pile direction)*

For Rail Fence, trace the A template 16 times, referring to Fig. 2 for direction of fabric pile.

For Two Triangles, trace ruler template, following Fig. 3 as a guide for measurements and for direction of pile. You will need 14 pieces. Note that template is reversed (R) for half the pieces.

3. Cut out pillow back and patchwork pieces, adding ¼" seam allowances. Cut out ruffle strips on the pencil lines.

Piece pillow top

4. Arrange patchwork pieces, right side up, to form design.

For Rail Fence, see Fig. 4.

For Two Triangles, see Fig. 5.

5. Pin two adjacent pieces, right sides together, along the seam line. One piece will have a wale running along the edge; pin with that side on top, using the wale to keep the line straight. Be sure each pin goes through pencil lines on both top and bottom pieces, and keep pins close together.

Join the seam, using a long machine stitch. Check after stitching to be sure you have kept on the pencil lines. Press seam open, and trim ends to eliminate bulk.

For Rail Fence, work on one quarter of the design at a time, pinning and stitching pieces together. Join the two top quarters and the two bottom quarters. Then join the two halves.

For Two Triangles, join pieces to form the two large triangles. Then join the two halves. The final seam of the design involves matching many seam lines, so you may want to baste the seam and repin it before stitching.

6. When patchwork design is completed, stitch around the outside on pencil lines to mark the seam lines. On one side, finish edge with a zigzag stitch or a second line of straight stitching. (This will be the pillow opening.)

Make ruffle (optional)

7. If you are making a ruffle, join the two strips, right sides together, to make a big ring. Be sure pile is running in the same direction on both strips.

Fold ring in half, bringing raw edges together, right side out. Pin along edges. Beginning about 1″ from a seam, fold the ring in half, then in quarters. Mark each fold with a pencil dot at the raw edge.

8. To stitch a gathering line, work on a quarter of the ring at a time. Set machine for a long stitch and loosen the tension. Use regular thread in the top of the machine and buttonhole twist in the bobbin. Stitch sections, but do not pull threads to gather until later.

9. Pin ring to edge of pillow top, right sides together; place a ruffle quarter mark at the center of each edge. Align stitching on ruffle with stitching on pillow top. (Folded edge of ruffle should be toward center of pillow.)

Divide each quarter section of ruffle in half and pin center to corner of pillow top.

Pull bobbin threads to gather, distributing fullness evenly along edges (Fig. 6); add extra fullness at each corner. Let ruffle curve slightly around corners. Pin, baste and stitch.

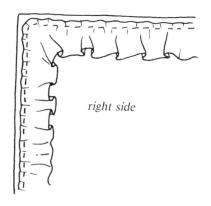

right side

Fig. 6 *Adding ruffle*

Assemble pillow

10. On pillow back, machine-stitch over pencil line on one side only (this will be the opening). Finish the same edge with a zigzag stitch, or make a second line of straight stitches close to the edge.

Pin pillow top to pillow back, matching finished edges for opening. If there is a ruffle, it will be sandwiched between the layers; pin ruffle gathers flat at corners and away from the stitching line.

Match seam lines of pillow top and back, and pin together.

You may want to baste, especially the corners. If you do, repin the seam before stitching.

Stitch with pillow top up. Begin on the edge that will be the opening, 1½″ from corner. Stitch three sides, and end with 1½″ of stitching on first edge. Lightly press seam open with tip of iron. To secure seam, use a zigzag stitch over the raw edges or add a second row of straight stitches about ⅛″ from the first line.

11. For inner pillow, stitch the muslin squares together with ¼″ seams; leave an opening for stuffing. Add fiberfill to make a firm, flat shape. Close opening.

12. Slip inner pillow into outer corduroy pillow cover. Close opening with slip stitches.

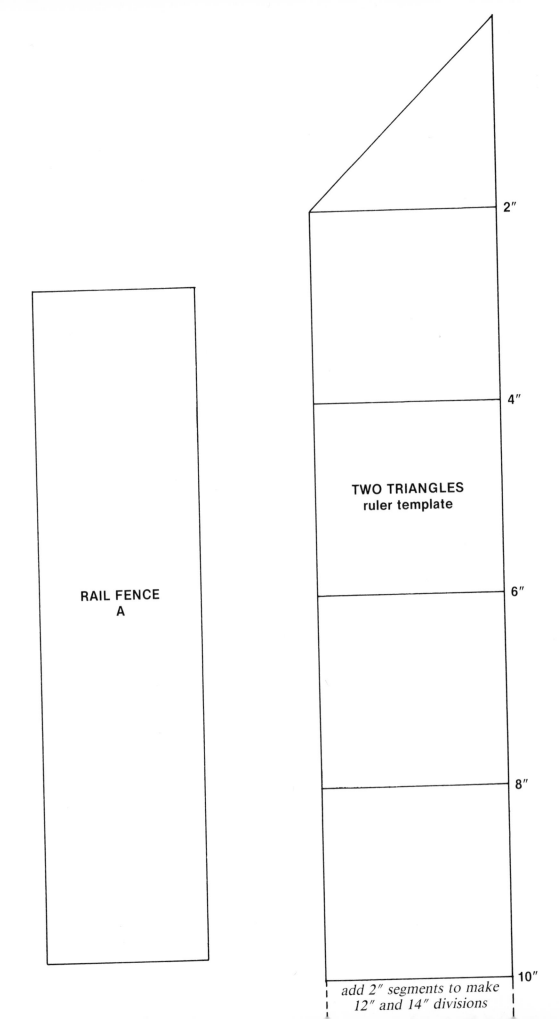

RAIL FENCE
A

TWO TRIANGLES
ruler template

2"

4"

6"

8"

10"

*add 2" segments to make
12" and 14" divisions*

Pieced Placemats

You can use a shortcut to make these placemats. First stitch long vertical strips together, then cut horizontal strips or shapes that will form the pattern.

This eliminates cutting out many little pieces. It also speeds up the stitching time because you have less than half as many seams to handle.

GENERAL MATERIALS
Follow directions for individual placemat, referring to directions below as needed.

To finish placemat
Place pieced front over back, right sides together, and pin edges. (On Eight Triangles, pin along pencil lines.) Trim back to match front, if necessary.

Smooth layers over batting and pin. Trim batting to same size. Stitch a ¼″ seam along the edge, leaving 5″ open for turning. (On Eight Triangles, stitch over pencil lines.)

Trim batting close to stitching. Trim seams and clip across corners. Turn placemat to right side, and close opening with slip stitches. Work seam to edge and press.

Baste layers together and quilt by hand or machine.

To make napkins
Cut fabric into four equal squares, 16″ to 18″ each. To make a double hem, turn each edge ¼″ to wrong side, then turn ¼″ again. Pin and press. Miter corner if desired. Stitch hem by hand or machine.

EIGHT TRIANGLES

(color photo, page 50)

Use two fabrics. If you put a striped fabric in the middle, it forms an interesting design when the triangles are stitched together. Just be sure you choose an even stripe (colors repeat the same in both directions). Finished mat is about 17″ across.

MATERIALS
(for four placemats and napkins)
1¾ yd. blue fabric with stripe, 44″ wide, for piecing and placemat backs (plus 1 yd. for napkins)
⅞ yd. blue fabric with white dots or print, 44″ wide, for piecing
Blue thread, for piecing
White thread (optional), for quilting
4 pieces thin polyester batting, 18″ square each

DIRECTIONS
(for one placemat and napkin)
For extra help with templates, stitching and quilting, see *Sewing Guides*, page 1.

Cut pattern and fabric
1. Trace triangle pattern, page 94, and make a template. Mark inside lines on template.

To make pattern for back, use a 20″-square sheet of paper and fold it in half. Begin at fold and trace triangle four times, butting sides together to make a half pattern (Fig. 1). Cut pattern on outside lines, and open paper to make full pattern.

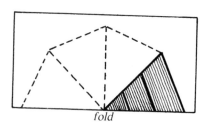

Fig. 1 *Drafting back pattern*

To mark fabric strips, make a template 3½" wide and about 10" long.

2. On wrong side of striped fabric, center the 3½" template over a stripe. Trace a 42"-long strip, moving the template along to get the length needed. Cut out on pencil lines. Seam allowances are included.

On wrong side of fabric with dots, place the 3½" template and trace two 42"-long strips (across the fabric width). Cut out on pencil lines. Seam allowances are included.

Place back pattern on wrong side of striped fabric and trace. Cut out, adding ¼" seam allowances.

Assemble placemat

3. Arrange the three fabric strips, with the striped fabric in the middle. Pin strips, right sides together, and stitch ¼" seams. Press seams toward center strip.

4. On wrong side of pieced fabric, place triangle template; match inside lines on template to seam lines on fabric. (If both lines do not match, use the top line only.) Trace one triangle. Rotate triangle half a turn and trace again (Fig. 2), leaving space for ¼" seam allowances.

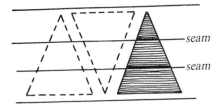

Fig. 2 *Tracing triangle template*

Continue rotating template and tracing until you have eight triangles. Cut out, adding ¼" seam allowances.

5. Arrange triangles to form design. On every other triangle, re-press seams so they will face away from the center strip.

(This will reduce bulk when joining triangles.)

Work with two triangles. Pin on pencil lines, right sides together; carefully match tips of triangles and seam lines on strips. Machine-stitch from outside edge to point at tip; do not stitch beyond tip.

Continue joining pairs of triangles. Then join pairs to make two halves. Finally, pin the two halves together, baste and stitch. Press all seams in the same direction.

6. To finish placemat, see *General Directions*. Quilt along seam lines on fabric strips and around outside, ¼" from edges.

7. To make napkin, see *General Directions*.

SQUARE STEPS

(color photo, page 50)

Use three fabrics to form this all-over checkered pattern. The sample mat has green, yellow and orange, and the finished size is about 12½x17".

MATERIALS
(for four placemats and napkins)

½ yd. medium green print, 44" wide, for piecing (plus 1 yd. for napkins)

1⅓ yd. bright yellow print, 44" wide, for piecing and placemat backs

½ yd. orange fabric, 44" wide, for piecing

Beige thread to blend with fabric colors, for piecing

Orange or other color thread, for quilting

4 pieces thin polyester batting, 13x18" each

DIRECTIONS
(for one placemat and napkin)
For extra help with templates, stitching and quilting, see *Sewing Guides*, page 1.

Cut pattern and fabric

1. Make a template 3" wide and about 10" long.

2. Place template on wrong side of fabric. On each of the three fabrics, mark three strips, 3x16" each; move template along to get the length needed. Cut out on pencil lines. Seam allowances are included.

On wrong side of yellow print, mark a 13x18" rectangle for placemat back and cut out. Seam allowances are included.

Assemble placemat

3. Arrange the nine strips vertically in color order—green print (at left), yellow print and orange. Repeat colors for the nine strips.

Pin the first two strips, right sides together, and stitch a ¼" seam. Press seam to one side. Add the third strip, stitch and press. Continue until all the strips are joined and the seams are pressed.

4. On the wrong side of the pieced fabric, place the 3" template. Mark five horizontal strips across the stitched pieces. Cut out on pencil lines. Seam allowances are included.

5. Arrange strips to form step pattern (Fig. 3). The finished mat has seven squares across each row. There will be two squares extending beyond the center pattern on all rows.

Carefully remove stitching and take away the extra squares. Press seam allowances on ends flat.

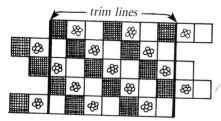

Fig. 3 *Arranging horizontal strips for Square Steps*

6. Pin the first two horizontal rows, right sides together, carefully matching corners of squares. Stitch a ¼″ seam, and press to one side. Continue adding each row, stitching and pressing in the same manner.

7. To finish placemat, follow *General Directions.* Quilt along selected seam lines or stitch diagonal lines through some of the squares.

8. To make napkin, see *General Directions.*

CHRISTMAS PLACEMAT

(color photo, page 50)

Only the colors make this a holiday placemat. You could use the design with any three colors—in prints or solids. There are just six seams to stitch for each pieced front, and you can use the machine to speed up quilting. Finished size is about 12½x17″.

MATERIALS

(for four placemats and napkins)
1¾ yd. print fabric, 44″ wide, for piecing and placemat backs (plus 1 yd. for napkins)
⅓ yd. green fabric, 44″ wide, for piecing
⅛ yd. red fabric, 44″ wide, for piecing
Green thread, for piecing and quilting
4 pieces of batting, 13x18″ each

DIRECTIONS

(for one placemat and napkin)
For extra help with templates, stitching and quilting, see *Sewing Guides,* page 1.

Cut patterns and fabric

1. Make three templates, about 10″ long each. Mark one 5″ wide, one 3″ wide and one 1½″ wide. Set the 3″ template aside.

2. Place templates on wrong side of fabric. On green fabric, use the 5″-wide template to mark a strip 16″ long; move template along to get the length needed. On red fabric, use the 1½″-wide template to mark a strip 16″ long. Cut out strips on pencil lines. Seam allowances are included.

On wrong side of print fabric, mark a rectangle 14½x16″ (for piecing). Cut out on pencil lines. Seam allowances are included.

On wrong side of print, also mark a 13x18″ rectangle for placemat back and cut out. Seam allowances are included.

Assemble placemat

3. Arrange the three 16″-long fabric pieces vertically in color order—green (at left), red and print. Pin the red strip to the green, right sides together, and stitch a ¼″ seam. Press to one side.

Pin the red strip to the print, right sides together, and stitch a ¼″ seam. Press to one side.

4. On the wrong side of the pieced fabric, place the 3″-wide template. Mark five horizontal strips across the stitched pieces. Cut out on pencil lines. Seam allowances are included.

5. Arrange strips to form pattern. Begin with middle strip (which uses full width of green fabric). Place strips above and below, so red pieces touch at corners. There will be extra fabric extending beyond the center pattern on all rows (Fig. 4).

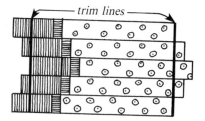

Fig. 4 *Arranging horizontal strips for Christmas Placemat*

On middle row, measure 2″ from the right end (on print fabric) and cut off. This leaves a middle strip 18″ long. Do not trim other strips until the seams are stitched.

6. Pin middle strip to strip above (second row); match corners of red pieces. Stitch a ¼″ seam and press to one side. Carefully trim both ends of second strip to match middle strip.

Pin and stitch top row strip to second row, matching corners on red pieces. Carefully trim left end on top row to correct size. Add fourth and fifth rows and trim in same manner.

7. To finish placemat, follow *General Directions.* To quilt by machine, stitch on top of all seam lines and ¼″ from outside edge.

8. To make napkin, follow *General Directions.*

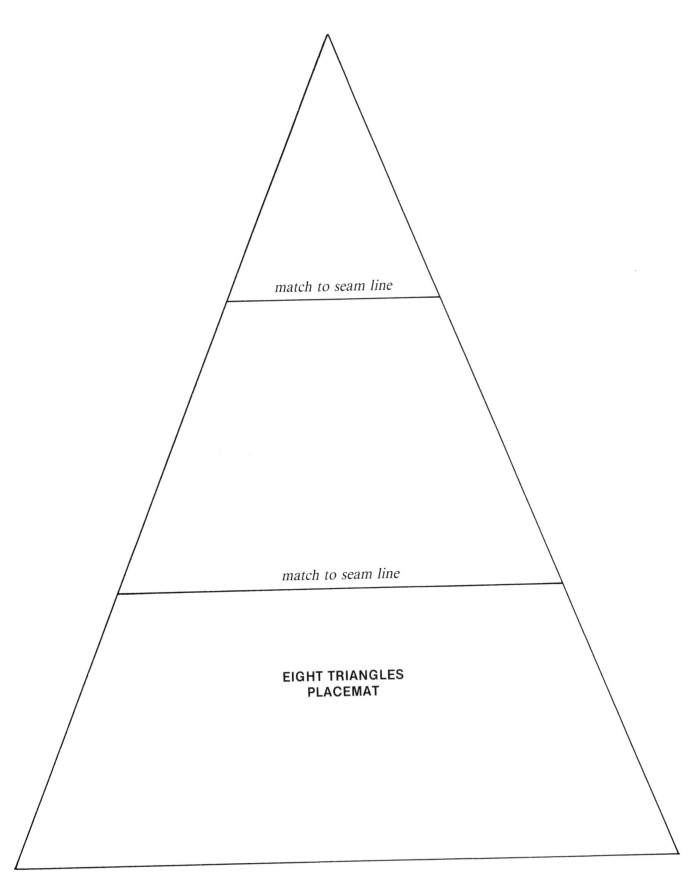

match to seam line

match to seam line

**EIGHT TRIANGLES
PLACEMAT**

Fabric Pictures

Each appliquéd picture has one or more stuffed pieces to make it three dimensional. Use one alone or mix it with other decorations to create an interesting wall grouping.

The picture is mounted on cardboard, then put in a frame. You should select a frame that has wire staples to hold the picture, rather than one with grooves for the picture to slide into place. (The padding may be too thick to fit in grooves.)

GENERAL DIRECTIONS

Follow directions for each picture, referring to the general guide below for mounting it.

To mount picture on cardboard

Place appliquéd background flat, right side down. On top, place batting rectangle in center, aligned with fold lines. Place cardboard on top of batting.

Fold background fabric along fold lines to back of cardboard. Pin fabric to cardboard on all sides, keeping grain of fabric straight; miter fabric at corners.

Spread white glue over fabric edges and rub with fingers to force glue through to cardboard. When glue is dry, remove and discard pins.

To finish, glue a rectangle of posterboard to cover back of picture.

RUFFLED FLOWER

(color photo, page 85)

The flower and leaves are padded and stitched, then attached to the 5x7″ picture. Use a striped fabric that looks like wallpaper for the background.

MATERIALS

Yellow fabric with stripe, 7x9″, for background (stripe should run along the 9″ length)
2 pieces red fabric, 6½″ square each, for flower
Medium green fabric, 4x9″, for leaves and stem
Dark green print, 3x6½″, for tablecloth
Red (with yellow) print scrap, for flowerpot
Thread to match fabrics
Thin polyester batting, 12″ square, for padding
Picture frame, 5x7″

1 piece firm cardboard and 1 piece posterboard, 5x7″ each
White glue

DIRECTIONS

For extra help with patterns, templates, stitching and appliqué, see *Sewing Guides,* page 1.

Cut patterns and fabric

1. Trace pattern for flower, page 98. Cut out the outside square only.

Trace pattern pieces for other appliqués and make templates for flowerpot and leaf.

Seam allowances will be added when cutting fabric.

2. On right side of red print, trace flowerpot. Cut out, adding ¼″ seam allowances.

On right side of dark green print, trace tablecloth. Cut out, adding ½″ seam allowances to side and bottom edges (as indicated on pattern), and ¼″ to top edge.

On green fabric (along a 4″ edge), mark a ½x3″ rectangle for stem, and cut out on pencil lines.

Fold remaining green fabric to make two layers, right side inside. On top, trace two leaves. Cut out a rectangle, 2x4″, around each.

Measure and cut a 5x7″ rectangle and a 6½″ square of batting.

Make flower and leaves

3. Lay the two red fabric squares flat, right sides together. Place layers over the 6½″ square of batting. On top, pin flower pattern to use as a stitching guide.

Begin at center A, and machine-stitch the broken (scalloped) line to the outside.

Carefully cut along the solid line, from outside B to A. Gently tear tracing paper away from stitching and discard. Trim batting close to stitching. Trim seam allowances along curves to under ¼″, and slash into each V point. Turn to right side and press lightly.

4. Pin raw edges of flower together. By machine or hand, stitch a gathering thread close to the edge, from A to B (Fig. 1).

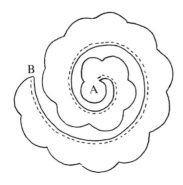

Fig. 1 *Stitching gathering thread*

Beginning at center, pull thread to gather and shape flower. Let scallops overlap raw edge, and make flower about 3″ in diameter. Hold edges in place with hidden stitches.

5. To make leaves, place each green rectangle over a rectangle of batting and pin. Stitch each leaf on pencil lines; leave bottom open.

Trim batting to stitching. Cut seam allowances along curves to under ¼″ and trim points. Cut seam allowance along bottom on pencil line. Turn each leaf to right side.

By hand, use green thread to quilt a line up the center of each leaf.

Add appliqués

6. Prepare background fabric. On wrong side of the striped fabric, mark a 5x7″ rectangle in the center. Lightly press a fold along each edge, following stripes on the sides. Open and baste along folds.

7. To prepare flat appliqués (flowerpot, and top seam on tablecloth), turn seam allowances to wrong side, baste and press.

8. Place tablecloth appliqué on right side of background, aligning pencil edge lines on tablecloth with folds on background. Pin in place and sew top seam of tablecloth with a hemming stitch.

To secure other edges, use matching thread and machine-stitch seam allowances to background fabric; use a zigzag if your machine has one. (This is outside the picture area.)

9. To prepare stem appliqué, fold long sides of the stem rectangle to meet at center, right side outside; press. (This makes the stem ¼″ wide.)

Center stem on background, just above the tablecloth, with stem parallel to stripes. Sew to background.

10. Center flower on stem, about ⅝″ from top fold of background. Attach with hidden stitches.

11. Position flowerpot so it is centered and about ½″ from bottom edge of picture. Pin in place.

12. Position leaves. Place the left leaf flat, right side down, so it is angled in pot. (See pattern for guideline.) Leaf should just overlap stem, and leaf tip should point to upper left corner of background. Pin to hold.

Place right leaf so it overlaps stem and first leaf, and the tip points to upper right corner. Pin to hold.

13. Sew base of leaves in place (under flowerpot). Appliqué flowerpot, adding a little stuffing before closing. (You can tear batting apart to make loose stuffing.)

Finish picture

14. To mount picture on cardboard and add posterboard backing, see *General Directions.*

15. Turn tip of each leaf downward, so it is about ½″ from side edge of picture and about even with top of flowerpot. Catch in place with hidden stitches.

16. Place picture in frame.

SURFING BEAR

(color photo, page 85)

The wave, surfboard and sun are appliquéd to the background. The bear is stitched separately, stuffed and added last. Finished picture is 8x10″.

MATERIALS

Blue and white gingham in small check, 10½x12½″, for background
Medium blue fabric, 4½x10″, for wave
2 pieces medium brown fabric, 6″ square each, for bear
Red fabric, 2x7½″, for surfboard
Yellow fabric scrap, for sun
Yellow felt scrap, for heart
White fabric scraps, for lining appliqués
Thread to match fabrics
Black and yellow embroidery floss
Thin polyester batting, 8x10″, for padding
Polyester fiberfill, for bear
Frame, 8x10″
1 piece firm cardboard and 1 piece posterboard, 8x10″ each
White glue

DIRECTIONS

For extra help with patterns, templates, stitching and appliqué, see *Sewing Guides*, page 1.

Cut patterns and fabric

1. Trace pattern pieces, page 99, and make templates. Seam allowances will be added when cutting fabric.

2. On right side of red fabric, trace surfboard template, face up. Cut out, adding ¼″ seam allowance.

On right side of blue fabric, trace wave, face up. On right side of yellow, trace sun, face up. Cut out, adding ½″ seam allowances to straight edges (as indicated on pattern) and ¼″ on other edges.

On white, trace sun and surfboard (for linings). Cut out on pencil lines.

On two layers of yellow felt, trace heart. Cut out on pencil line.

Make bear

3. Place brown fabric squares flat, right sides together. On top, trace bear template, face down.

Transfer head outline to right side of top layer by basting along pencil lines with brown thread. On right side, copy lines for face.

Embroider face with black floss, using a stem stitch for mouth and ear, and a satin stitch for eye and nose.

Pin top layer to bottom layer, right sides together. Machine-stitch around bear, leaving an opening on one side. Cut out, adding a seam allowance just under ¼″. Slash seam allowance to stitching at V points and along inside curves. Turn to right side and press lightly. Stuff bear loosely, keeping it flat. Close opening with slip stitches.

4. Stitch yellow heart layers together with yellow floss and a blanket stitch.

For neck "chain," cut a 4″ length of yellow floss (all six strands) and tie around bear's neck; keep knot in back and trim thread ends. Attach felt heart to chain with a loop of floss.

Add appliqués

5. Stay-stitch appliqué edges to be turned under (surfboard, top of wave and sunrays); straight edges on wave and corner of sun are left flat. Slash to stitching at V points and along inside curves, turn seam allowances to wrong side and baste. (Place linings against wrong side of surfboard and sun before basting.)

6. Prepare background fabric. On the wrong side of the blue check, mark an 8x10″ rectangle in the center. Lightly press a fold along each edge, keeping checks in straight lines. Open and baste along folds.

7. Place blue wave on right side of background, aligning pencil edge lines on wave with folds on background. Pin in place and sew top line of wave with a hemming stitch.

8. Position surfboard along top of wave, about 1″ from left fold line on checked fabric. Tilt board upward at front. Sew in place with a hemming stitch.

9. Position sun in upper left corner, aligning edge lines on sun with fold lines on checked fabric. Sew along sunrays with a hemming stitch.

10. To secure straight edges of wave and sun, use matching thread and machine-stitch seam allowances to checked fabric; use a zigzag if your machine has one. (This is outside the picture area.)

Finish picture

11. To mount picture on cardboard and add posterboard backing, see *General Directions*.

12. Position bear on background. Center bear, with feet on surfboard. Pin, and sew in place with long hidden stitches; catch bottom layer only, leaving edges of bear free.

13. Place picture in frame.

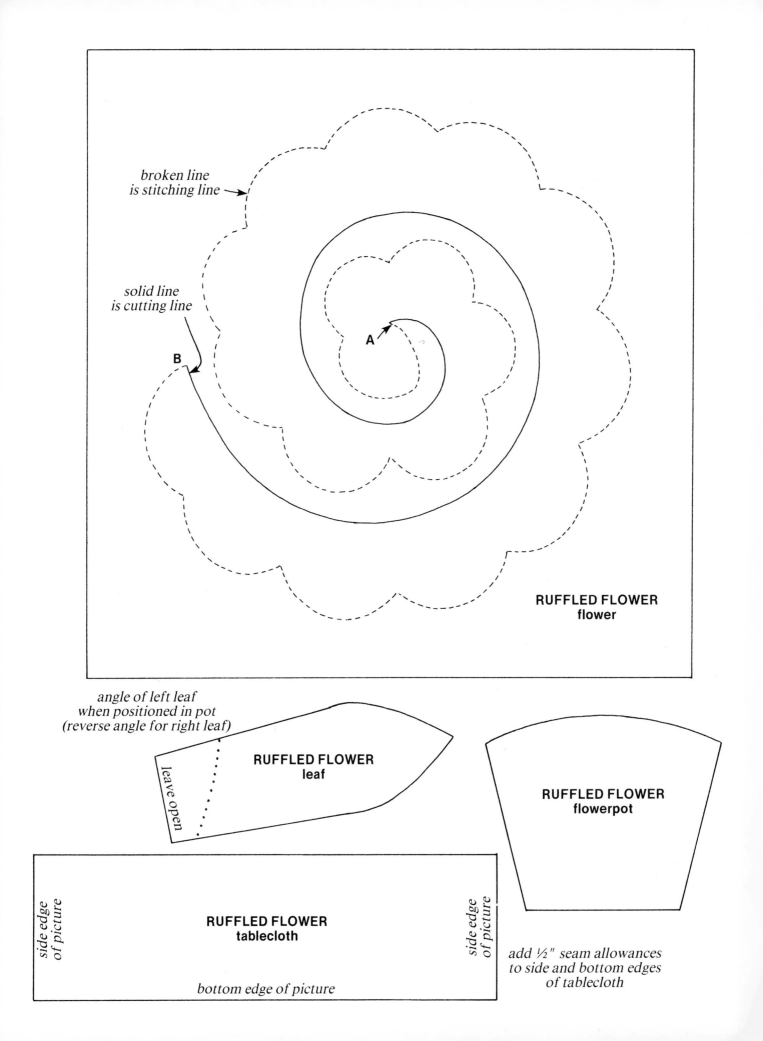

broken line
is stitching line →

solid line
is cutting line

A

B

RUFFLED FLOWER
flower

angle of left leaf
when positioned in pot
(reverse angle for right leaf)

leave open

RUFFLED FLOWER
leaf

RUFFLED FLOWER
flowerpot

side edge
of picture

side edge
of picture

RUFFLED FLOWER
tablecloth

bottom edge of picture

add ½" seam allowances
to side and bottom edges
of tablecloth

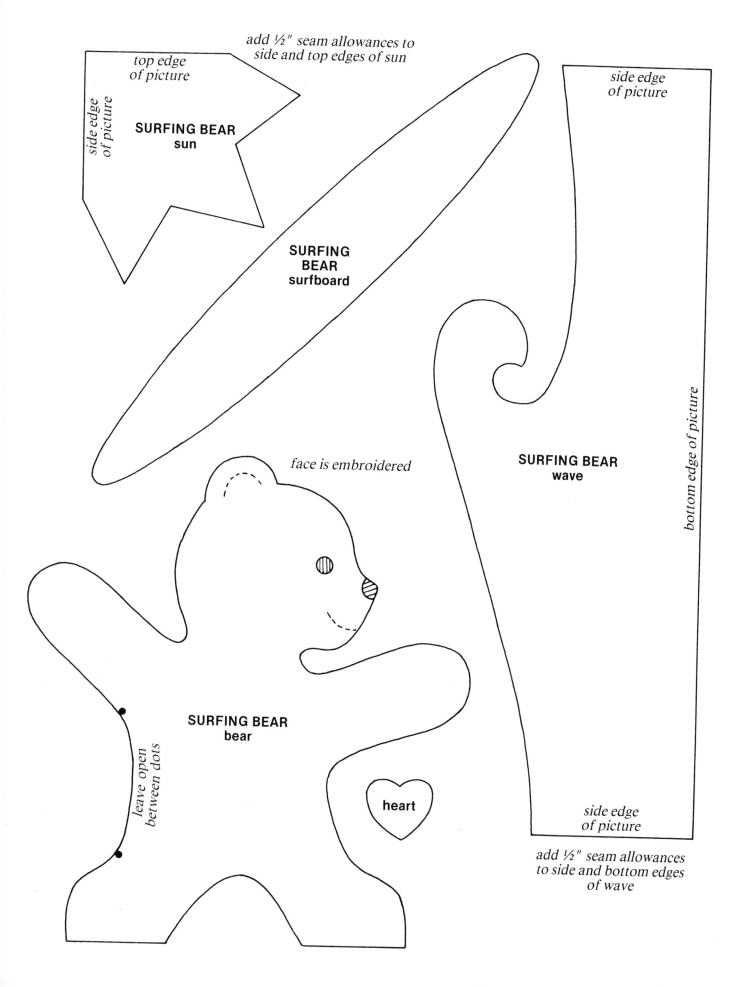

add ½" seam allowances to
side and top edges of sun

top edge
of picture

side edge
of picture

SURFING BEAR
sun

**SURFING
BEAR**
surfboard

side edge
of picture

face is embroidered

SURFING BEAR
wave

bottom edge of picture

SURFING BEAR
bear

leave open
between dots

heart

side edge
of picture

add ½" seam allowances
to side and bottom edges
of wave

Picture Pincushions

Here's a novel way to keep pins handy. Hang picture pincushions on the wall—right in plain sight. Put one in the bathroom, and another in the bedroom or laundry area.

Each picture has one or more parts made double and stuffed firmly to serve as the pincushion. For instance, the Apple Tree has a fat treetop and the Cat Face has stuffed jowls. If you use printed fabrics for these sections, the pins will blend in with the design.

The finished picture is padded with polyester batting and framed in an embroidery hoop. To hang, place a decorative hook on the wall, and slip the tightening screw on the hoop over the hook.

APPLE TREE

(color photo, page 47)

The apple, tree trunk and grass are flat appliqués. The three treetop units are firmly stuffed to hold pins.

MATERIALS

Light blue fabric: 11″ circle, for background; 9″ circle, for backing
Light green fabric, 4x8″, for grass
Medium green print (with some red), 6½x16″, for treetop
Dark brown fabric (solid or with small dots), 3x3½″, for tree trunk
Red fabric, 2½″ square, for apple
Thread to match fabrics
Blue or beige buttonhole twist, for gathering
Dark green and black embroidery floss
Thin polyester batting, 10″ square
Polyester fiberfill
7″ embroidery hoop

DIRECTIONS

A compass will help you draw the circles. For extra help with patterns, templates, stitching and appliqué, see *Sewing Guides*, page 1.

Cut patterns and fabric

1. Trace pattern guide, page 104. Go over lines with a pen to make them darker.

Trace separate patterns for grass, tree trunk and apple, and make templates. Trace patterns A, B and C for treetop and cut out. Seam allowances will be added when cutting fabric.

2. Place templates for flat appliqués on right side of fabric, face up. On light green, trace grass. On brown, trace tree trunk. On red, trace apple. Cut out fabric, adding ¼″ seam allowances.

For treetop pieces, fold green print in half, right side inside. On top, place pieces A, B and C, face up; leave space for ¼″ seam allowances. Trace and cut out fabric, adding ¼″ seam allowances.

Place the 9″ circle of light blue fabric over the batting and cut batting to match.

Assemble picture

3. Center the 11″ light blue circle over pattern guide. Pin or tape fabric edges to hold in

place. With a pencil, lightly trace outside circle. Mark top of pattern with a dot on the circle. Trace top line of grass and section of tree trunk above grass. Remove pattern.

4. Turn raw edge of the 11″ circle ¼″ to the wrong side and baste. Set machine for gathering (long stitch, loose tension). Use buttonhole twist in the bobbin and regular thread on top. Begin at the bottom of the picture on the right side, and machine-stitch over the folded edge. Do not pull threads to gather until later.

5. Prepare flat appliqués (grass, tree trunk, apple). Stay-stitch at V points and along inside curves. Slash seam allowances at V points and inside curves almost to the stitching. Turn all seam allowances to the wrong side on pencil lines, baste and press.

6. Position grass on background, using pencil line for top edge as a guide. Place tree trunk and apple in place. (Lay tracing paper pattern on top if you need to check positions.) Pin appliqués and baste.

Sew all appliqué edges with a hemming stitch. Begin with the grass. Then sew tree trunk in place. Sew apple last, tucking in a little fiberfill before closing.

7. For trim, go over top seam on grass with two strands of dark green floss and a blanket stitch. Embroider apple stem with two strands of black floss and a few chain stitches.

8. Make treetop pieces. Stitch each unit, right sides together; leave opening between dots. Before turning, separate the layers on each unit; fold top layer to form dart. Pin and stitch dart. Turn unit to right side.

Stuff each unit firmly with fiberfill. Use a crochet hook handle or other small tool to pack the fiberfill. Close opening with slip stitches.

9. Arrange treetop units in position (Fig. 1), with darts at back. A overlaps C at left; B overlaps A and C at center. Pin unit B to A to hold (stab pins through layers).

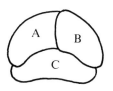

Fig. 1   *Joining treetop units*

Carefully lift A and B and sew together on the back; use a double strand of thread in a long needle, and take long stitches.

Pin the A/B unit to C and sew together on the back. On the front, catch units together where necessary, using hidden stitches. Then set treetop aside.

10. Stack circle layers. Lay the 9″ blue circle flat, right side down. Add the 9″ batting circle. On top, center the appliquéd circle, right side up. Pin layers together and baste.

By machine, use a long stitch and sew over the pencil circle on the top (appliquéd) layer.

11. Center layers over inside circle of hoop. Fit outside circle of hoop in place, and pull fabric to make top layer taut. (Outside edge of grass will be hidden by hoop.)

Position treetop section and pin in place (stab pins through layers). Carefully remove fabric from hoop. Using a double strand of thread and a long needle, sew from the back to catch treetop to background. Sew along the center of each treetop unit; take diagonal stitches through the layers as you work across each unit (Fig. 2). When finished, background fabric should not pucker when it is fitted in hoop.

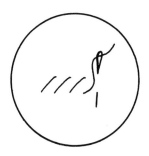

Fig. 2   *Sewing stuffed section to background*

12. Replace fabric in hoop with tightening screw at top. Pull fabric taut.

To gather outside circle, pull bobbin threads. Gather edge into a tight inner circle on back, pull thread ends to the wrong side and tie to secure.

CAT FACE

(color photo, page 47)

It could be a panther or just a house cat, but those fat jowls offer you a handy pincushion.

MATERIALS
Light brown fabric: 10″ circle, for background; 8″ circle, for backing
Tan fabric, 6½x17″, for face, ears and mouth section
Rusty brown fabric, 5x10″, for nose/eyebrows
Tan and brown print, 5x11″, for jowls and ear linings
Thread to match fabrics
Beige buttonhole twist, for gathering
Black embroidery floss

Thin polyester batting, 9"
  square
Polyester fiberfill
6" embroidery hoop

DIRECTIONS
Face is lined with the same fabric to eliminate see-through. A compass will help you draw the circles.

For extra help with patterns, templates, stitching and appliqué, see *Sewing Guides*, page 1.

Cut patterns and fabric
1. Trace pattern pieces, page 103, and make templates. Seam allowances will be added when cutting fabric.

2. Place templates on right side of fabric. On tan, trace face; use paper pattern to mark lines for eyes. Also trace two ears. Cut out fabric, adding ¼" seam allowances.

On single layer of tan fabric, trace a second face and cut out on pencil line. (This is the lining.)

For two layers, fold each fabric, right side inside. On tan, trace mouth section. On print, trace ear and jowls. On rusty brown, trace nose/eyebrows. Cut out fabric, adding ¼" seam allowances.

Place the 8" light brown circle over batting and cut batting to match.

Stitch the parts
3. For face appliqué, place lining on wrong side of face piece. Turn raw edge of face to wrong side (over lining) along pencil line and pin. Baste and press.

4. To make each ear, pin a tan piece to a print piece, right sides together. With tan side up, stitch along pencil lines on two sides; leave bottom curve open. Trim seam and clip off point. Turn to right side and press lightly.

5. Stitch jowl layers, right sides together; leave opening for turning. Trim seams, turn to right side and press lightly.

Stuff each curved side firmly. Use a crochet hook handle or other small tool to pack the fiberfill. Stuff center portion lightly, and close opening with slip stitches. Use a double strand of thread and sew a line up the center; catch both layers of fabric and gather the line slightly.

6. Stitch layers of mouth section, right sides together; leave an opening for turning. Turn to right side and press lightly.

On right side, use paper pattern to mark mouth line. Embroider top layer, using two strands of black floss and a chain stitch. Stuff section lightly and close opening with slip stitches.

7. To join mouth and jowls, fit mouth section between jowls. Pin and sew together on the back; use a double strand of thread in a long needle and take long stitches.

8. Stitch the nose/eyebrow layers, right sides together; leave an opening for turning. Turn to right side and press lightly. On front layer, mark curve at top of nose.

Stuff nose lightly, keeping it flat. Pin fabric layers together along curve at top of nose. By hand, stitch the curved line, catching both fabric layers. Stuff eyebrows very lightly and close opening with slip stitches.

Assemble picture
9. In the center of the 10" light brown fabric circle, draw a 6½" circle with a light pencil line.

10. Turn raw edge of the 10" circle ¼" to the wrong side and baste. Set machine for gathering (long stitch, loose tension). Use buttonhole twist in the bobbin and regular thread on top. Begin at the bottom of the circle on the right side, and machine-stitch over the folded edge. Do not pull threads to gather until later.

11. Center face appliqué on the large fabric circle and pin in place. Position ears, with raw edges under edge of face. Baste around face. Attach face with a hemming stitch, catching ears in the stitches.

12. Finish eyes. Embroider outlines, using two strands of black floss and a chain stitch.

On black felt, use template to trace two eye pupils. Cut out. Center a black felt pupil in each eye and attach with black thread, sewing over the felt edges.

13. To outline the face, embroider around edge, using two strands of black floss and a chain stitch.

14. Stack circle layers. Lay the 8" brown circle flat, right side down. Add the 8" batting circle. On top, center the 10" appliquéd circle, right side up. Pin layers together and baste.

By machine, use a long stitch and sew over the pencil circle on the top (appliquéd) layer.

15. Position nose/eyebrow unit on face, matching top of unit to top center of face. Attach with a hemming stitch; begin under an eyebrow (at nose), go across top, and end under other eyebrow at nose. Leave nose free.

16. Position jowls/mouth unit on face, with lower edge of mouth section over bottom edge of chin. Pin in place (stab pins through layers).

Carefully turn layers over and catch stuffed units to background. Use a double strand of thread in a long needle. Sew along the center of the jowls and the mouth section; take diagonal stitches through the layers as you work across each section (see Fig. 2 under Apple Tree). When finished, background fabric should not pucker when it is fitted into hoop.

17. Place fabric layers over inside circle of hoop. Fit outside circle of hoop in place, with tightening screw at top of picture. Pull fabric taut. (Machine stitching on circle should be hidden by hoop.)

To gather outside circle, pull bobbin threads. Gather edge to form a tight inner circle on the back, pull thread ends to the wrong side and tie to secure.

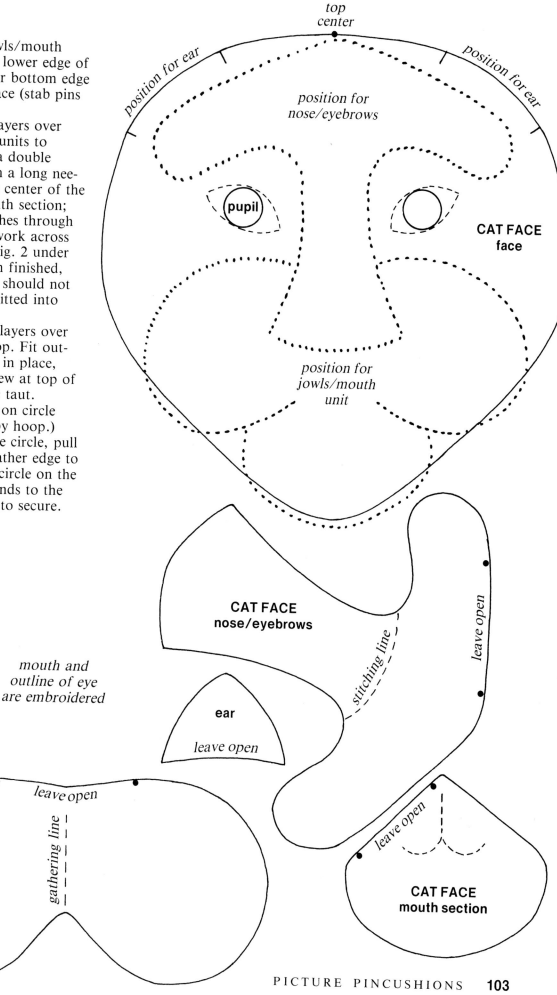

top center

position for ear

position for ear

position for nose/eyebrows

pupil

CAT FACE
face

position for jowls/mouth unit

CAT FACE
nose/eyebrows

mouth and outline of eye are embroidered

stitching line

leave open

ear
leave open

CAT FACE
jowls

leave open

gathering line

leave open

CAT FACE
mouth section

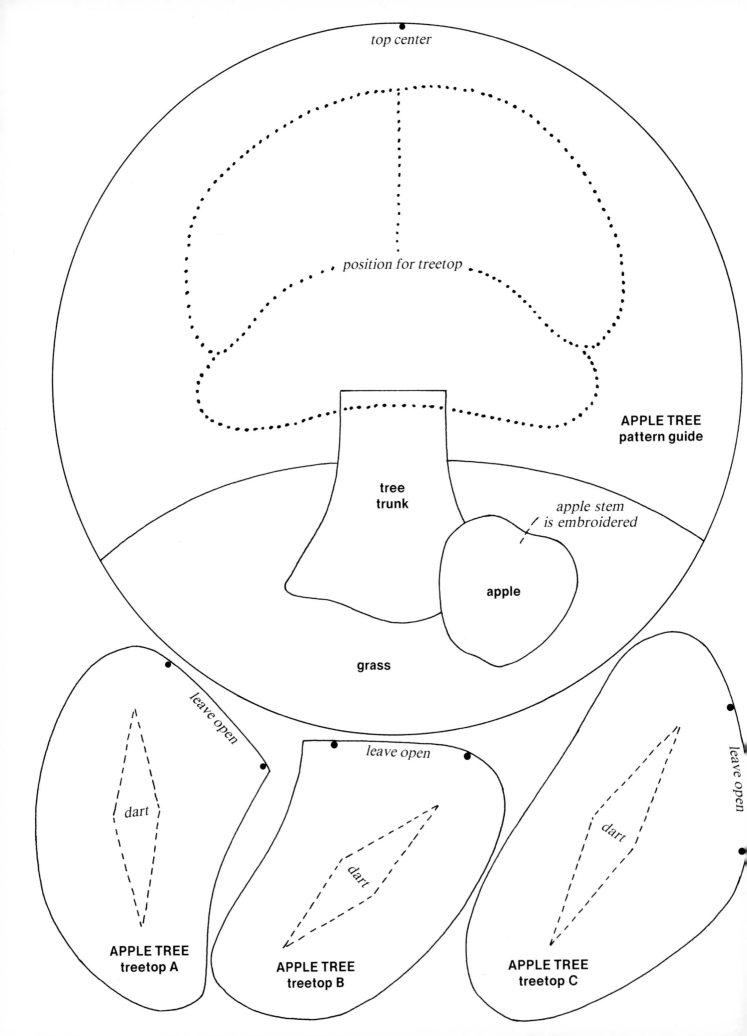

top center

position for treetop

APPLE TREE
pattern guide

**tree
trunk**

*apple stem
is embroidered*

apple

grass

leave open

dart

APPLE TREE
treetop A

leave open

dart

APPLE TREE
treetop B

leave open

dart

APPLE TREE
treetop C

Circus Ornaments

Let the fun-filled world of the circus add a happy note to your home. For year-round enjoyment, hang a few of these ornaments from a dowel or bare tree branch, painted white.

For Christmas, stitch one ornament as a gift for a special friend, or complete the whole set for your Christmas tree.

The ornaments are made of felt, sewed together with embroidery floss and blanket stitches. To save time, you could use regular thread and small running stitches.

GENERAL DIRECTIONS

Follow directions for each ornament, referring to the guide below for making a loop. For extra help with patterns, templates and stitching, see *Sewing Guides,* page 1.

To make loop for hanging

Thread needle with 8" of gold metallic thread. Take one stitch at top of ornament and remove needle. Hold both ends of thread together and tie a knot, making a loop about 3" long. Clip ends of thread. Use ornament hook for hanging finished ornament on tree.

TRAINED SEAL

(color photo, page 121)

Make the seal's body and fold the tail end forward. Add two front flippers and a ball.

MATERIALS

2 pieces blue felt, 5½x6½" each, for seal
Fuchsia felt, 2½x5", for ball
Bright pink felt, 2½x5", for trims
Embroidery floss in black and colors to match felt
Polyester fiberfill
Gold metallic thread and ornament hook, for hanging

DIRECTIONS

Join felt layers with matching floss and a blanket stitch. Use two strands of floss for all stitching.

Cut patterns and felt

1. Trace pattern pieces for seal and ball, page 111, and make templates. Seam allowances are included.

2. Place templates on two layers of felt. On blue, trace body and two front flippers. On fuchsia, trace ball.

On single layer of pink felt, trace collar and two stars.

Cut out on pencil lines.

Assemble seal

3. Mark an eye on the outside of each body layer. Embroider, using black floss and a satin stitch.

4. Join body layers, stuffing lightly before closing. Fold tail end of body to front and secure with a few hidden stitches.

5. Join layers for the two front flippers, tucking a little fiberfill in each unit before closing. Position a flipper on each side of body and attach with hidden stitches.

6. For whiskers, use two strands of black floss. Take a tiny stitch over edge of felt, leaving a ½" tail. Take a second stitch over the first, pull the needle through the loop formed to make a knot. Clip thread, leaving a ½" tail. Repeat to complete three whisker stitches.

7. For collar, work a line of blanket stitches along the scalloped edge. Position collar around seal's neck and stitch ends together. Attach top edge of collar to seal with blanket stitches.

8. For ball, center and stitch a star to the outside of each layer. Then join layers, stuffing ball lightly; leave a small opening at bottom.

9. Insert seal nose extension in ball. Finish stitching ball, catching each layer to seal.

10. To add loop for hanging, follow *General Directions.*

TRAPEZE LADY

(color photo, page 120)

Stitch the two main units—the head/arms and the suit. Put them together and add the trapeze.

MATERIALS
2 pieces pale pink felt, 3x5½″ each, for arms and head
2 pieces bright pink felt, 5x5½″ each, for suit
Yellow and bright blue felt scraps, for trims
Embroidery floss in red, bright blue and colors to match felt
Polyester fiberfill
3″ black chenille stem, for trapeze
13″ bright blue yarn
Ornament hook (optional)

DIRECTIONS
Join felt layers with matching floss and a blanket stitch. Use two strands of floss for all stitching.

Cut patterns and felt
1. Trace pattern pieces for Trapeze Lady, page 112, and make templates. Seam allowances are included.

2. On two layers of bright pink felt, trace suit. On single layer of yellow, trace hair front and hair back. On single layer of blue, trace star.
Cut out on pencil lines.

3. On two layers of pale pink felt, trace head/arms pattern and copy lines for face.
Before cutting, embroider face. For mouth, use red floss and a stem stitch. For eyes, use bright blue and a satin stitch; end with one straight stitch for nose.
Place embroidered felt over second layer and cut out on pencil line.

Assemble lady
4. Join head/arms layers, stitching between large dots on face and chest; leave top of head and lower edge open.
Pin hair in place. Attach hair front to face. Join outside edges of hair. Finally, attach lower edge of hair back to back of head.
Lightly stuff head, arms and chest. Embroider hair band with pink floss and a stem stitch.

5. On suit front, stitch star trim. Then join suit layers, stitching from large dot at one underarm to dot on opposite underarm; leave top open. As you close each leg at the knee, stuff foot and lower leg lightly with fiberfill. When finished, stuff legs and body.

6. Position head/arms unit inside suit. Add stuffing where needed. Stitch suit to arms and neck at front and back.

7. For trapeze, tie ends of blue yarn to ends of chenille stem. Position figure on bar, folding hand over center of bar. Secure with hidden stitches.

8. Hang ornament from the blue yarn, or add an ornament hook.

TRAPEZE MAN

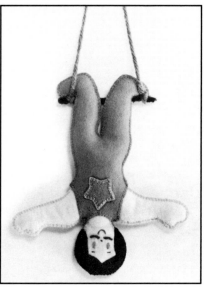

(color photo, page 120)

Finish the figure. Then give him a trapeze made from a chenille stem and yarn.

MATERIALS
2 pieces pale pink felt, 4x7″ each, for arms and head
2 pieces fuchsia felt, 4½x5½″ each, for suit
Black and bright blue felt scraps, for trims
Embroidery floss in red, black, bright blue and colors to match felt
Polyester fiberfill
3″ black chenille stem, for trapeze
13″ bright blue yarn
Ornament hook (optional)

DIRECTIONS

Join felt layers with matching floss and a blanket stitch. Use two strands of floss for all stitching.

Cut patterns and felt

1. Trace pattern pieces for Trapeze Man, page 113, and make templates. Seam allowances are included.

2. On two layers of fuchsia felt, trace suit. On single layer of black, trace hair front and hair back. On single layer of blue, trace star.

Cut out on pencil lines.

3. On two layers of pale pink felt, trace head/arms pattern and copy lines for face.

Before cutting, embroider face. For mouth, use red floss and a stem stitch. For eyes, use bright blue and a satin stitch. For mustache, use black floss and two lines of stem stitch, close together; end with a single stitch for each eyebrow and the nose.

Place embroidered felt over second layer and cut out on pencil lines.

Assemble man

4. Join head/arms layers, stitching between large dots on face and chest; leave top of head and lower edge open.

Pin hair in place. Attach hair front to face. Join outside edges of hair. Finally, attach lower edge of hair back to back of head. Lightly stuff head, arms and chest.

5. On suit front, stitch star trim. Then join suit layers, stitching from large dot at one underarm to dot on opposite underarm; leave top open. As you close each foot, stuff lightly with fiberfill. When finished, stuff legs and body.

6. Position head/arms unit inside suit. Add stuffing where needed. Stitch suit to arms and neck at front and back.

7. For trapeze, tie ends of blue yarn to ends of chenille stem. Position figure on trapeze, with feet overlapping bar at each end. Secure with hidden stitches.

8. Hang ornament from the blue yarn, or add an ornament hook.

BALANCING BEAR

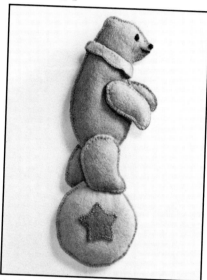

(color photo, page 120)

Complete the body section. Make and attach four legs and the ball.

MATERIALS

2 pieces bright green felt, 5x5½" each, for bear
Bright pink felt, 5x6½", for ball and collar
Blue felt scrap, for stars
Embroidery floss in black and colors to match felt
Polyester fiberfill
Gold metallic thread and ornament hook, for hanging

DIRECTIONS

Join felt layers with matching floss and a blanket stitch. Use two strands of floss for all stitching.

Cut patterns and felt

1. Trace pattern pieces for bear and ball, page 114, and make templates. Seam allowances are included.

2. Place templates on two layers of felt. On green, trace body, two front legs and two hind legs. On pink, trace ball.

On single layer of pink felt, trace collar. On single layer of blue, trace two stars.

Cut out on pencil lines.

Assemble bear

3. Mark an eye and mouth on the outside of each body layer. Embroider with black floss, using a satin stitch for eyes and a stem stitch for mouth.

4. Join body layers, stuffing lightly before closing.

Add nose with black floss. Work a buttonhole stitch over the felt edges, catching both layers.

5. Join layers for each leg unit, adding a little fiberfill before closing.

6. For ball, center and stitch a star to the outside of each layer. Then join layers, stuffing ball lightly.

7. Pin hind legs to body and to ball, letting a foot just overlap ball on each side. Pin front legs in position. Secure all units with hidden stitches.

8. For collar, work a line of blanket stitches along the scalloped edge. Position collar around bear's neck and stitch ends together. Attach top edge of collar to bear with blanket stitches.

9. To add loop for hanging, follow *General Directions.*

SNAKE CHARMER

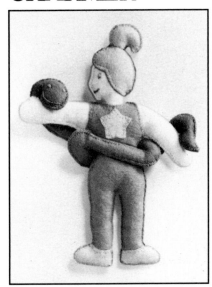

(color photo, page 120)

Stitch the snake and wrap it around the charmer's body.

MATERIALS
2 pieces pale pink felt,
    3½x6½″ each, for head
    and arms
2 pieces orange felt, 3x5½″
    each, for suit
2 pieces bright green felt,
    3½x7½″ each, for snake
Bright yellow felt, 4x6″, for
    trims
Embroidery floss in red, bright
    blue and colors to match felt
Polyester fiberfill
Gold metallic thread and orna-
    ment hook, for hanging

DIRECTIONS
Join felt layers with matching
floss and a blanket stitch.
Use two strands of floss for all
stitching.

Cut patterns and felt
1. Trace pattern pieces for
charmer and snake, page 115,
and make templates. Seam
allowances are included.
2. Place templates on two
layers of felt. On pale pink,
trace head/arms pattern. On
orange, trace suit. On green,
trace snake. On yellow, trace
hair and two shoes (one
reversed).
On single layer of yellow,
trace star.
Cut out on pencil lines.

Assemble charmer and snake
3. Mark an eye and mouth on
the outside of each pink face
layer. Embroider, using blue
floss with a satin stitch for eyes
and red floss with a stem stitch
for mouth.
4. Join head/arms layers,
stitching between large dots on
head and chest; leave top of
head and lower edge open.
Pin top edges of hair together
and join between large dots;
leave lower edge open.
Position hair on head; add a
little fiberfill to top and sides of
hair and pin in place. Stitch
hair to face at front and back.
Lightly stuff head, arms and
chest. Embroider hair band
with orange floss and a stem
stitch.
5. On suit front, stitch star
trim. Then join suit layers,
stitching from large dot on one
underarm to dot on opposite
underarm; leave top open.
Lightly stuff legs and body.
6. Position head/arms unit
inside suit, adding stuffing
where needed. Stitch suit to
arms and neck at front and
back.
7. For each shoe, join layers
on outside edges; leave top
open. Stuff toe, slip shoe over
leg and stitch in place.
8. Stitch snake layers together, adding stuffing as you
close each section. Using orange
floss, embroider mouth with a
stem stitch and eyes with a satin
stitch.
9. Add snake to charmer, letting snake head overlap hand.
Take top section of snake
behind charmer's body, middle
section across front of body,
and lower section across back
of body. Let end of tail overlap
opposite hand. Use hidden
stitches to catch snake's head
and tail in place.
10. To add loop for hanging,
follow *General Directions.*

DANCING ELEPHANT

(color photo, page 120)

The two bottom legs are cut as
part of the body. Sew and stuff
the top legs separately, then
attach.

MATERIALS
2 pieces blue felt, 6x7″ each,
    for elephant
Orange felt, 6″ square, for trims
Bright yellow felt, 3x4″, for
    trims
Embroidery floss in black and
    colors to match felt
3 lengths of blue yarn, 5″ each,
    for tail
Polyester fiberfill
Gold metallic thread and orna-
    ment hook, for hanging

DIRECTIONS
Join felt layers with matching
floss and a blanket stitch.
Use two strands of floss for all
stitching.

Cut patterns and felt
1. Trace pattern pieces for
elephant, blanket and stool,
page 116, and make templates.
Seam allowances are included.

2. Place templates on two layers of felt. On blue, trace body, one front leg, one hind leg and two ears. On orange, trace stool.

Next, use single layers of felt. On orange, trace blanket (bottom layer) and two stars. On yellow, trace blanket (top layer), one stool top and two stars.

Cut out on pencil lines.

Assemble elephant

3. Mark an eye on the outside of each body layer. Embroider, using black floss and a satin stitch.

4. Begin joining body layers at dot behind head. As you close the trunk, stuff lightly with fiberfill. Continue stitching; stuff body lightly before closing. Join layers for legs and ears, tucking a little fiberfill in each unit before closing.

5. Position legs on top layer of body and attach with hidden stitches. Pin an ear to each side of body, and attach along the front edge with hidden stitches.

6. For tail, thread each 5″ length of yarn in a needle; take a stitch and draw yarn halfway through edge of felt. Divide yarn into three units and braid to make a 1″ length. With blue floss, wrap and tie end of braid to secure. Trim yarn ends to leave a ½″ tassel.

7. For blanket, center yellow top layer on orange bottom layer and attach with yellow floss. At each end, center an orange star and attach with orange floss.

To fringe outside edge of blanket, clip orange layer almost to yellow layer at ⅛″ intervals.

Fold blanket in half, position on elephant's back and attach with hidden stitches.

8. For stool, position yellow stool top on one layer of orange stool; stitch along the curve with yellow floss. Center

and stitch a yellow star to the outside of each stool layer. Then join stool layers, stuffing lightly before closing.

9. Position elephant on stool, with feet overlapping stool top about ¼″. Attach with hidden stitches.

10. To add loop for hanging, follow *General Directions.*

CLOWN JUGGLER

(color photo, page 121)

Join the head and suit, then add the hands and feet. Finally, give this clown three hoops for his juggling act.

MATERIALS

2 pieces red felt, 4½x5½″ each, for suit and nose
2 pieces pale pink felt, 2½x3″ each, for head
2 pieces orange felt, 3″ square each, for hair
Yellow felt, 5″ square, for trims
Green, blue and purple felt scraps, for hoops
Embroidery floss in bright blue and colors to match felt
Polyester fiberfill
Gold metallic thread and ornament hook, for hanging

DIRECTIONS

Join felt layers with matching floss and a blanket stitch. Use two strands of floss for all stitching.

Cut patterns and felt

1. Trace pattern pieces for clown and hoop, page 117, and make templates. Seam allowances are included.

2. Place templates on two layers of felt. On red, trace suit. On yellow, trace two hands (one reversed) and two shoes (one reversed). On blue, green and purple, trace one hoop each.

Next, use single layers of felt. On yellow, trace star. On orange, trace hair front and hair back.

Cut out on pencil lines.

3. On two layers of pale pink felt, trace head pattern and copy lines for face.

Before cutting, complete face. For nose, cut a ¼″ circle of red felt and attach with blanket stitches. Embroider other features, using red floss with a stem stitch for mouth and bright blue with a satin stitch for eyes.

Place embroidered felt over second pink layer and cut out on pencil line.

Assemble clown

4. Join head layers, stitching between large dots on face and neck; leave top of head and lower edge open.

5. Pin hair in place. Stitch hair front to face. Join outside edges of hair. Lightly stuff head and neck; add a bit of stuffing between hair back and head. Stitch lower edge of hair back to back of head.

6. On suit front, stitch star trim. Then join suit layers, stitching from large dot at neck, around arms and legs to dot on opposite side of neck. Stuff suit lightly.

7. Position head inside suit. Add stuffing where needed. Stitch suit to neck at front and back.

8. For each hand, stitch layers together; leave opening between dots. Add stuffing, slip hand over arm and stitch in place.

9. For each shoe, join layers on outside edges; leave top open. Stuff toe, slip shoe over leg and stitch in place.

10. Stitch layers of each hoop together, closing outside edges first; add stuffing and close inside edges.

Pin a hoop to each hand. Pin third hoop to top of hoop on left side (see photo for position). Attach hoops with hidden stitches.

11. To add loop for hanging, follow *General Directions*.

LEAPING LION

(color photo, page 121)

Complete the lion and the hoop, and sew them together.

MATERIALS
2 pieces bright yellow felt, 3½x7″ each, for body
2 pieces orange felt, 3x3½″ each, for mane
2 pieces bright blue felt, 2½x4½″ each, for hoop
2 pieces red felt, 4x6″ each, for flame
Embroidery floss in black and colors to match felt
Polyester fiberfill
Gold metallic thread and ornament hook, for hanging

DIRECTIONS
Join felt layers with matching floss and a blanket stitch. Use two strands of floss for all stitching.

Cut patterns and felt
1. Trace pattern pieces for lion, hoop and flame, page 118, and make templates. Seam allowances are included.

2. Place templates on two layers of felt. On yellow, trace body. On orange, trace mane. On blue, trace hoop. On red, trace flame.

Cut out on pencil lines.

Assemble lion
3. Mark an eye and mouth on the outside of each body layer. Embroider with black floss, using a satin stitch for eyes and a stem stitch for mouth.

4. Join body layers, leaving section under mane (between large dots) open. Stuff tail and legs.

5. Pin mane together at top. Position on each side of body and attach. Stuff body lightly and add a little fiberfill between mane and body. Close top of mane.

6. Add nose, using black floss. Work a close buttonhole stitch over felt edges, catching both layers.

7. Add tail fringe, using six strands of orange floss. Work over both layers of felt. Take one stitch and pull through, leaving a ¾″ tail. Take a second stitch over the first one, pull the needle through the loop formed to make a knot. Clip thread to leave a ¾″ tail. Make about 10 knots close together. Finally, trim tail fringe to about ½″.

8. For hoop, stitch outside edges of red flame together. Stuff lightly and close inside edges with running stitches (these will be covered). Stitch inside edges of blue hoop together. Position blue hoop on red flame, letting hoop overlap the flame on both sides. Attach with a blanket stitch.

9. Slip hoop over lion so lion is headed downward. Attach with hidden stitches.

10. To make loop for hanging, follow *General Directions*.

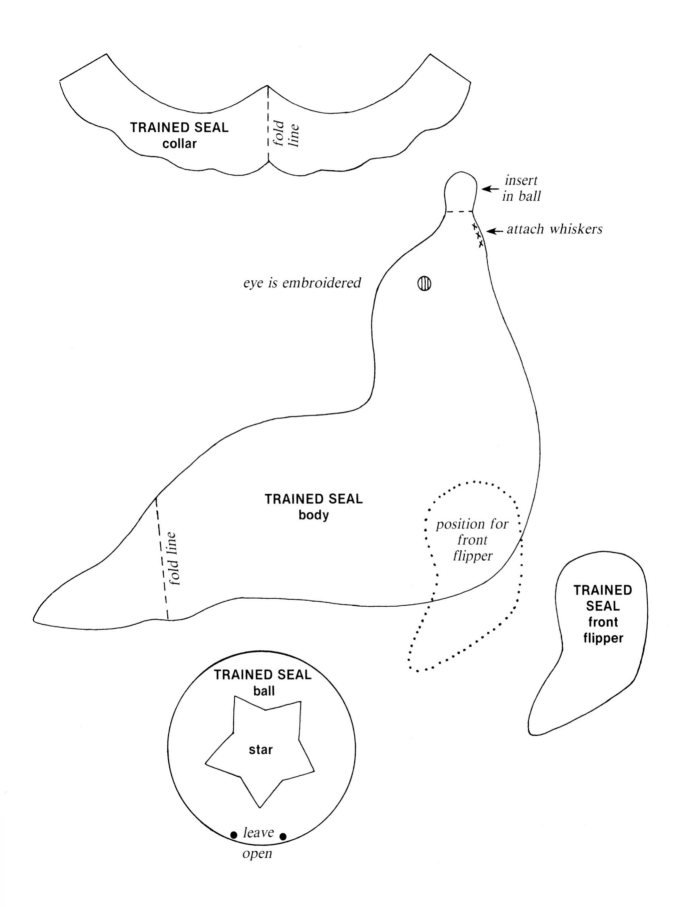

TRAINED SEAL
collar

fold line

insert in ball ←

attach whiskers ←

eye is embroidered

TRAINED SEAL
body

fold line

position for front flipper

TRAINED SEAL
front flipper

TRAINED SEAL
ball

star

leave open

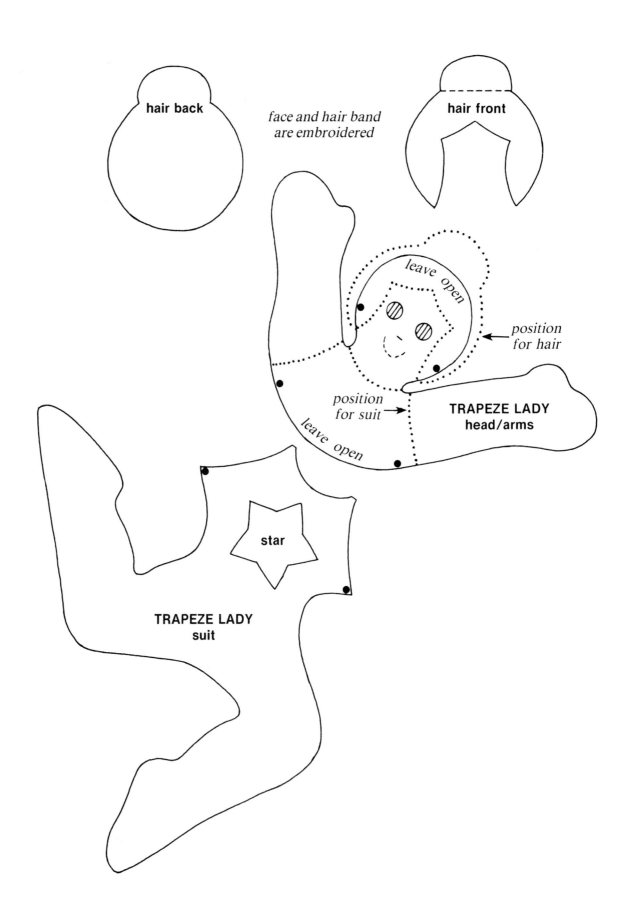

hair back

face and hair band
are embroidered

hair front

leave open

position
for hair

position
for suit

leave open

TRAPEZE LADY
head/arms

star

TRAPEZE LADY
suit

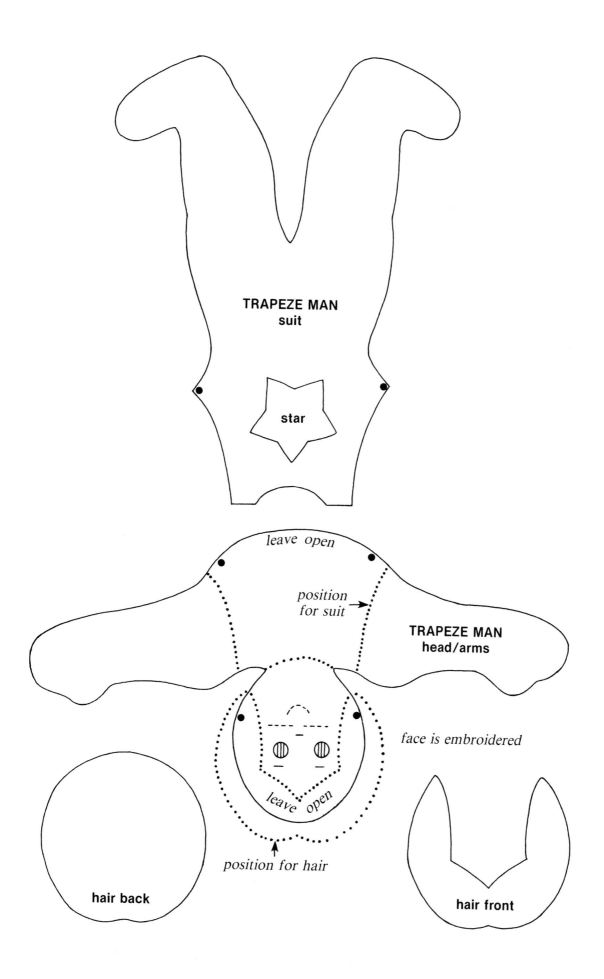

TRAPEZE MAN
suit

star

leave open

position
for suit

TRAPEZE MAN
head/arms

face is embroidered

leave open

position for hair

hair back

hair front

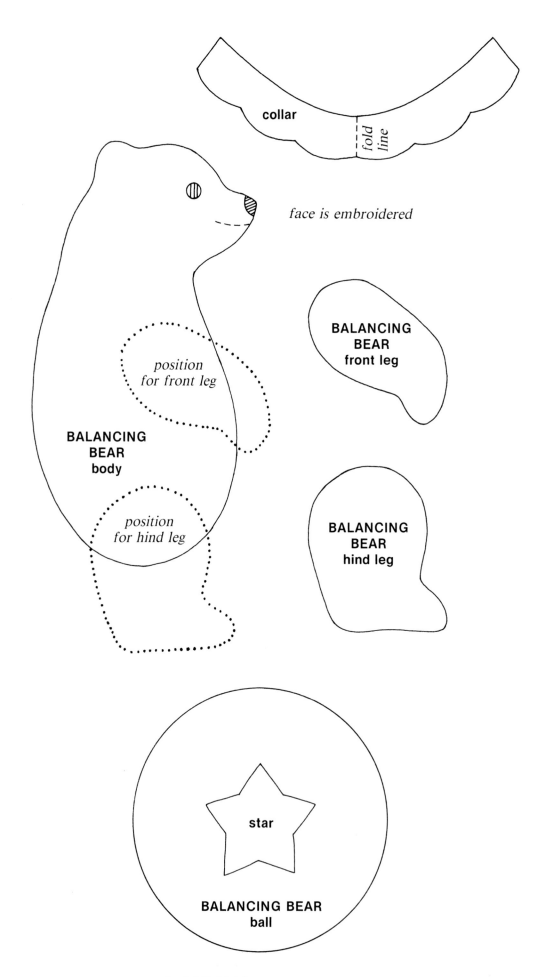

collar

fold line

face is embroidered

BALANCING BEAR front leg

position for front leg

BALANCING BEAR body

position for hind leg

BALANCING BEAR hind leg

star

BALANCING BEAR ball

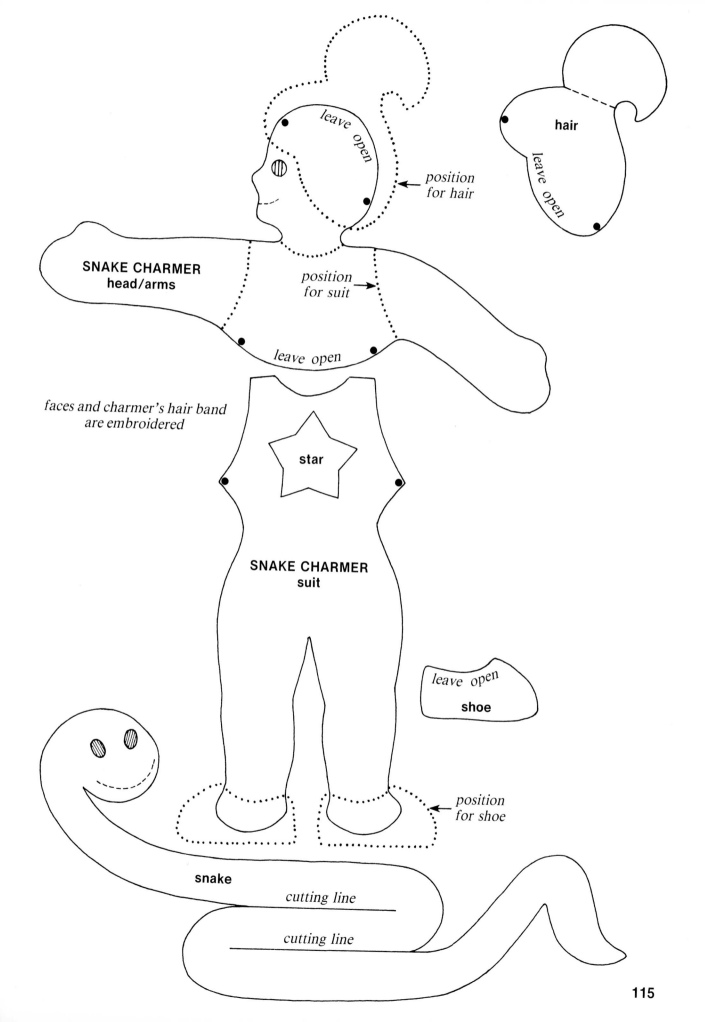

hair

leave open

leave open

position
for hair

SNAKE CHARMER
head/arms

position
for suit

leave open

faces and charmer's hair band
are embroidered

star

SNAKE CHARMER
suit

leave open

shoe

position
for shoe

snake

cutting line

cutting line

115

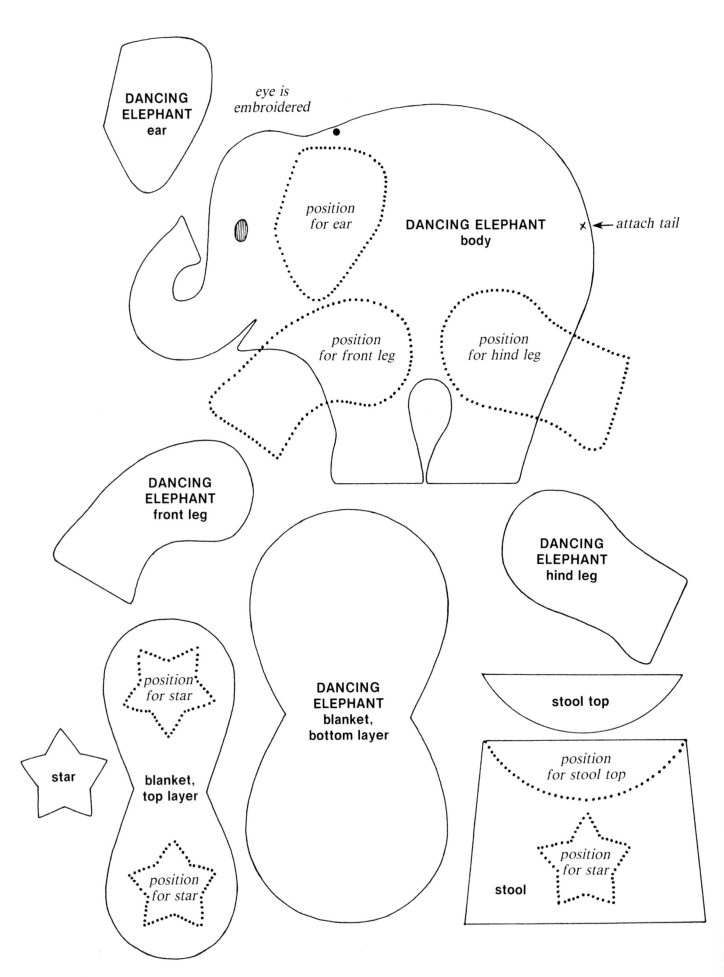

DANCING
ELEPHANT
ear

*eye is
embroidered*

*position
for ear*

DANCING ELEPHANT
body

x ← *attach tail*

*position
for front leg*

*position
for hind leg*

DANCING
ELEPHANT
front leg

DANCING
ELEPHANT
hind leg

*position
for star*

DANCING
ELEPHANT
blanket,
bottom layer

stool top

star

blanket,
top layer

*position
for star*

*position
for stool top*

*position
for star*

stool

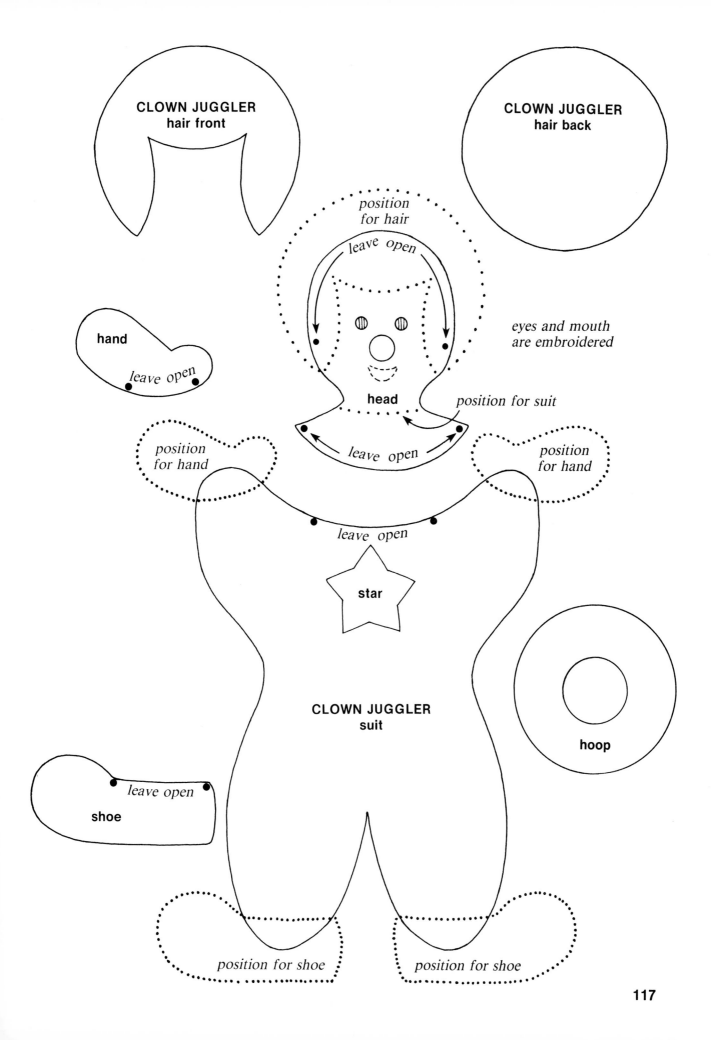

CLOWN JUGGLER
hair front

CLOWN JUGGLER
hair back

*position
for hair*

leave open

*eyes and mouth
are embroidered*

hand

leave open

head

position for suit

*position
for hand*

leave open

*position
for hand*

leave open

star

hoop

leave open

shoe

CLOWN JUGGLER
suit

position for shoe

position for shoe

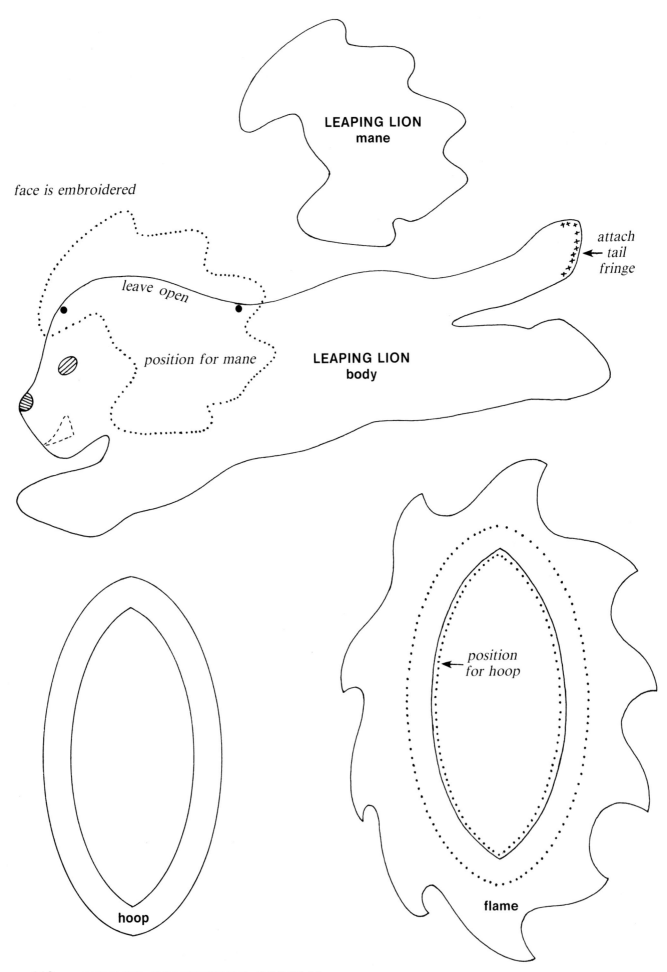

LEAPING LION
mane

face is embroidered

leave open

position for mane

LEAPING LION
body

attach
tail
fringe

position
for hoop

hoop

flame

Wall hangings (page 133) for a child's room can be made from quilt block designs used in the Playtime Quilt. Shown from the top are Batter Up, Teddy Bear and Swinging High.

One or more of these felt Circus Ornaments (page 105) can help decorate a small space on the wall or add a custom look to a Christmas tree. On the opposite page, clockwise from the top, are Trapeze Lady, Trapeze Man, Dancing Elephant, Balancing Bear and Snake Charmer. On this page, clockwise from above, are Trained Seal, Leaping Lion and Juggling Clown.

Playtime Quilt

This quilt is a picture story of a boy and girl and their cat and dog. One block (Peaceful Moment) shows the youngsters dressed up, standing still for a picture. The rest of the blocks show them the way they look most of the time—in action.

The quilt has 13 appliquéd blocks (two are double size), set with sashing. The finished quilt size is 77x113", which fits a standard twin mattress (39x75"), with a 19" overhang on all sides. (Full outside border does not show in photo.)

Center panel of blocks and sashing is 38x72". You can make the quilt smaller or larger by changing the border sizes.

Colors in the sample quilt are mainly rust, green, blue, red and yellow. You can use the same colors, which are listed in the directions as a guide, or you can choose your own colors. Be sure to check your scrap bag for appliqué fabrics and trims.

Any one of the blocks also can be appliquéd and quilted alone for a wall hanging. Directions for this variation follow instructions for making the quilt.

MATERIALS
(Yardage for fabric 44" wide)
1 yd. white fabric, for background blocks, appliqués and appliqué linings
⅞ yd. pale green fabric, for background blocks
⅞ yd. pale blue fabric, for background blocks
½ yd. medium blue fabric, for background in Gone Fishin' block and for appliqués
1⅛ yd. light rust fabric with small dots, for sashing
9⅝ yd. medium rust print, for outside border, backing and appliqués
2½ yd. medium green print, for middle border* and appliqués
2⅛ yd. dark blue print, for inside border and appliqués
¼ yd. bright yellow fabric
¼ yd. peach fabric
Medium blue print, 8x21", for girl's dress and bonnet
Fabric scraps: orange, red, yellow-green, light green, medium green, bright rust (for boy's hair), medium brown (for dog), dark blue, black, yellow print, red print, medium blue fabric with white dots, dark brown print
Thread to match fabrics
Quilting thread in white or colors to match fabrics
Embroidery floss in black, bright blue, medium green, red and brown
1⅛ yd. ruffled lace, ¼" wide

1 pkg. polyester batting, 90x108"
(With this amount of fabric, you can cut each border strip in one section. If you cut each green print border strip in two sections and piece it, you will need only 1½ yd. of fabric.)

DIRECTIONS
For extra help with fabric preparation, patterns, templates, stitching, appliqué and quilting, see *Sewing Guides*, page 1.

Prepare fabric
1. Preshrink and press all fabric if quilt is to be washed.
2. Cut squares from border fabrics to use for appliqués. From medium green print, cut a 20" square. From dark blue print, cut a 15" square. From medium rust print, cut a 9" square. Set aside larger sections for borders.
3. Measure blocks, allowing ½" seam allowances.
On wrong side of white fabric, mark five rectangular blocks, 10x12" each.
On wrong side of pale green fabric, mark one block 12x22", and two blocks, 10x12" each.
On wrong side of pale blue fabric, mark four blocks, 10x12" each, and mark one block 10x13".
On wrong side of medium blue fabric, mark one block 10x13".

Cut out blocks, adding ½″ seam allowances. Use leftover fabric for appliqués.

Make blocks

Follow these general steps for each block, referring to the individual block for additional fabrics and directions.

4. On tracing paper, draw a rectangle the size of the block. Center paper on pattern in book and trace design, joining sections along broken lines if necessary. Go over pattern lines with a pen to make the lines darker.

5. Lay fabric block, right side up, over traced pattern, with center of design in center of block. Lightly trace pattern outline onto fabric with pencil (Fig. 1). These lines will be a guide for placing appliqué pieces.

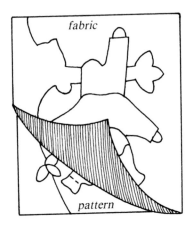

Fig. 1 *Marking placement lines on fabric*

Note: If you can't see pattern lines through the fabric, go on to Step 6 and make templates. Then position templates on background fabric and trace around them. (Place tracing paper pattern over fabric and slide templates into position under pattern.)

6. Make templates. Place tracing paper pattern over oak tag board (or similar weight material). Slide carbon paper between layers and go over pattern lines with a pencil. Remove tracing and carbon papers and cut out around pattern shapes.

If any template shapes are to be divided, carefully cut them apart to make separate pattern pieces.

7. To make appliqués, place templates on right side of fabric, face up, and trace with pencil. Cut out, adding ¼″ seam allowances.

As a general guide, use:
Peach for faces, hands
   and legs on girl and boy;
Bright yellow for girl's hair
   and cat;
Medium brown (body), white
   (face) and black (ears)
   for dog;
Bright rust for boy's hair.
   Check individual blocks for additional fabrics.

8. Prepare appliqué pieces. On any raw edge that will be turned under, stay-stitch and slash V points and inside curves. Turn seam allowance to wrong side and baste, rolling stitching out of sight. *Note:* Any seam that will be covered by another appliqué is left flat. When necessary, line appliqués to prevent see-through (see page 4).

9. Position appliqué pieces on background block, pin and baste. Sew in place with a hemming stitch, beginning with the bottom layer.

10. Embroider faces and other design lines. For all blocks, work with two strands of floss. Use red floss for mouths on girl and boy, bright blue for girl's eyes, brown for boy's eyes and black for all other lines unless otherwise noted.

Use a satin stitch for eye pupils and animal noses, a single straight stitch for noses on boy, girl and sun, and a stem stitch for all other face lines.

11. To make a separate bow (for Peaceful Moment, Dog with Bow Tie, Cat with Bonnet and Teddy Bear), cut two fabric rectangles to sizes indicated under the individual block.

Fold the larger rectangle in half, right side inside, with the long edges together. Stitch a ¼″ seam on the long edge. Turn tube to right side, position seam in center of one side and press flat.

Form bow by folding raw edges to overlap ¼″ at center, with seam hidden inside. By hand, catch ends at center and press bow flat. Sew a line up center of bow, pull thread to gather, and secure (Fig. 2).

Fig. 2 *Gathering center of bow*

On the smaller rectangle, fold the long edges to overlap the center, right side outside. Press. Wrap the fabric strip around bow, with raw ends overlapping on back of bow (Fig. 3). Sew along overlap.

Stitch bow in place, catching center of bow and outside edges to block.

Fig. 3 *Adding center strip*

SWINGING HIGH

(Row 1, block 1)

Rope lines for the swing extend to the edge of the block, and they are embroidered in a chain stitch.

Additional materials
Red fabric, for girl's suit
Yellow print, for heart trim
Medium green print, for cap
Dark blue print, for swing
Light green fabric, for shoes

Additional directions
Trace full pattern, pages 134-135, joining sections on broken lines. For background, use a 10x12″ white block.
To embroider rope lines, use medium green floss and a chain stitch.

KITE

(Row 1, block 2)

Combine four fabrics for the kite and tail. The kite string will be extended and embroidered later.

Additional materials
For kite and ties on kite tail: medium green print, yellow print, red print and dark blue print

Additional directions
Draw a 10x12″ rectangle and trace pattern, page 136. For background, use a 10x12″ pale blue block. See photo, page 122, for position of colors.
To embroider kite tail, use red floss and a chain stitch. Do not embroider kite string until sashing is added.

KITE FLYING

(Row 2, block 3)

This block is set diagonally below the kite. After the two top rows of blocks are joined with sashing, you can connect the kite string and embroider one continuous line.

Additional materials
Medium green fabric, for boy's pants
Medium green print, for shirt
Dark blue fabric, for cap
Yellow fabric, for shoes

Additional directions
Draw a 10x12″ rectangle and trace pattern, page 137. For background, use a 10x12″ pale blue block.
To outline shoes, use medium green floss and a stem stitch. Do not embroider kite string until later.

TEDDY BEAR

(Row 1, block 3)

The teddy bear has a separate bow which is attached to the neckband.

Additional materials
Orange fabric, for teddy bear
Medium blue fabric, for bear's neckband and bow
Dark blue print, for girl's suit
Red fabric, for girl's shoes

Additional directions
Draw a 10x12″ rectangle and trace pattern, page 138. For background, use a 10x12″ pale green block.
To embroider band on girl's hair, use bright blue floss and a chain stitch.
To make separate bow for the bear, cut two rectangles of medium blue fabric—one 2½x4½″ and one 1x1¾″. Then follow directions in Step 11.

BATTER UP

(Row 2, block 1)

The boy in the sample quilt wears a yellow suit and shoes, but you could substitute the colors of your home team.

Additional materials
Yellow fabric, for boy's suit and shoes
Medium green fabric, for cap, sleeves and socks
White fabric, for baseball
Dark brown print, for bat

Additional directions
Draw a 10x12″ rectangle and trace pattern, page 139. For background, use a 10x12″ pale blue block.
To embroider lines on ball, use red floss and a feather stitch. For lines on suit, use green floss and a chain stitch.
To separate green pieces (on sleeves, socks and cap), you can use yellow floss and a stem stitch. To outline shoes, use medium green floss and a stem stitch.

JUMPING ROPE

(Row 2, block 2)

The curved rope line is embroidered in a chain stitch.

Additional materials
Yellow print, for girl's shirt
Orange fabric, for pants
Medium blue fabric with white dots, for cap
Dark blue fabric, for shoes

Additional directions
Draw a 10x12″ rectangle and trace pattern, page 140. For background, use a 10x12″ white block.
To embroider jump rope, use bright blue floss and a chain stitch.

(Row 3, block 1)

(Row 3, block 2)

This double block shows the youngsters and pets in a quiet pose. There also are two bluebirds in the air.

The girl's bonnet is edged in ruffled lace. The bonnet bow and the boy's bow tie are made separately and attached to the block.

Additional materials
Medium blue print, for girl's dress and bonnet
Ruffled lace, for bonnet
Medium blue fabric, for bonnet bow, girl's shoes and birds
White fabric, for boy's pants
Yellow fabric, for boy's shirt and shoes
Medium green print, for boy's tie
Red fabric, for cat's collar

Additional directions
Draw a 12x22″ rectangle and trace full pattern, pages 141-143; join sections on broken lines. For background, use the 12x22″ pale green block.

Pin edge of ruffled lace under outside (turned) edge of bonnet. Then sew bonnet to background, catching lace with the stitches.

With black floss, use a stem stitch to outline legs on cat and dog, and a chain stitch to embroider their leashes. Use bright blue floss and a chain stitch for straps on girl's shoes. Use medium green floss and a chain stitch for boy's belt. Use yellow floss for birds' eyes.

To make separate bows for trim, cut two fabric rectangles for each bow. For boy's tie, use medium green print; cut one piece 3½x5½″ and one piece 1x2″. For bow on girl's bonnet, use medium blue fabric; cut one piece 2½x4½″ and one piece 1x1¾″.

Stitch and form each bow, following directions in Step 11.

The doghouse seems a good place to hide from this red bird.

Additional materials
Dark blue print, for doghouse
Pale blue fabric, for doghouse doorway
Red fabric, for bird
Medium blue fabric, for girl's cap
Yellow print, for girl's shirt
Medium green fabric, for boy's cap
Medium green print, for boy's shirt

Additional directions
Draw a 10x12″ rectangle and trace pattern, page 146. For background, use a 10x12″ white block.

To embroider bird's legs and to outline cat's head (optional), use black floss and a stem stitch.

TREE CLIMBING

(Row 4, block 1)

Both cat and girl are up a tree. You may want to cut the tree appliqué in one piece and sew the other appliqués on top. Use a lining if necessary to prevent the dark tree fabric from showing through lighter fabrics (see page 4).

Additional materials
Dark brown print, for tree
Medium green print, for girl's shirt
Orange fabric, for pants
Medium blue fabric, for shoe
Medium green fabric, for leaves

Additional directions
Trace full pattern, pages 144-145. For background, use a 10x12″ pale blue block.

On tree appliqué, straight edges should be left flat. These will be caught in seams when block is stitched to sashing.

To embroider bands on girl's hair, use medium green floss and a chain stitch.

SKATEBOARD

(Row 4, block 2)

The boy looks free as a bird as he rolls along.

Additional materials
Medium rust print, for boy's shirt
Dark blue fabric, for pants
Dark blue print, for cap
Bright rust fabric, for shoes
Dark brown print, for skateboard

Additional directions
Draw a 10x12″ rectangle and trace pattern, page 147. For background, use a 10x12″ white block.

DOG WITH BOW TIE

(Row 5, block 1)

The dog is dressed up in a green cape and the boy's bow tie. A little red bird checks the outfit.

Additional materials
Medium green print, for bow tie
Light green fabric, for cape
Red fabric, for bird

Additional directions
Draw a 10x12″ rectangle and trace pattern, page 148. For background, use a 10x12″ white block.

To embroider bird's legs, use black floss and a stem stitch.

To make separate bow for tie, cut two rectangles of medium green print—one 5x8″ and one 1½x2½″. Then follow directions in Step 11.

CAT WITH BONNET

(Row 5, block 2)

The cat wears the girl's lace-edged bonnet. The blue bow is made separately and added last.

Additional materials
Medium blue print, for bonnet
Ruffled lace, for bonnet
Medium blue fabric, for bonnet bow

Additional directions
Draw a 10x12" rectangle and trace pattern, page 149. For background, use a 10x12" pale green block.

Place edge of ruffled lace under outside (turned) edge of bonnet. Then sew bonnet to background, catching lace with the stitches.

To make separate bow for bonnet, cut two rectangles of medium blue—one 4½x7" and one 1¼x2½". Then follow directions in Step 11.

GONE FISHIN'

(Rows 4 & 5, block 3)

The background for this double block is divided in half, with pale blue above and medium blue below. There's a smiling sun in the sky, and three fish surround a fat worm in the water.

Additional materials
Red fabric, for boat
Yellow print, for boy's shirt
Dark blue fabric, for boy's cap
Yellow fabric, for sun
Yellow, white and yellow-green
   fabric, for the three fish
Orange fabric, for worm

Additional directions
Draw a 10x26" rectangle and trace full pattern, pages 150-152; join sections on broken lines.

To make the double block for background, stitch the 10x13" pale blue rectangle to the 10x13" medium blue rectangle along the 10" edges, right sides together. Press seam allowances to the darker blue side.

To embroider fishing pole, use bright blue floss and a chain stitch. For fishing line, use black floss and a stem stitch.

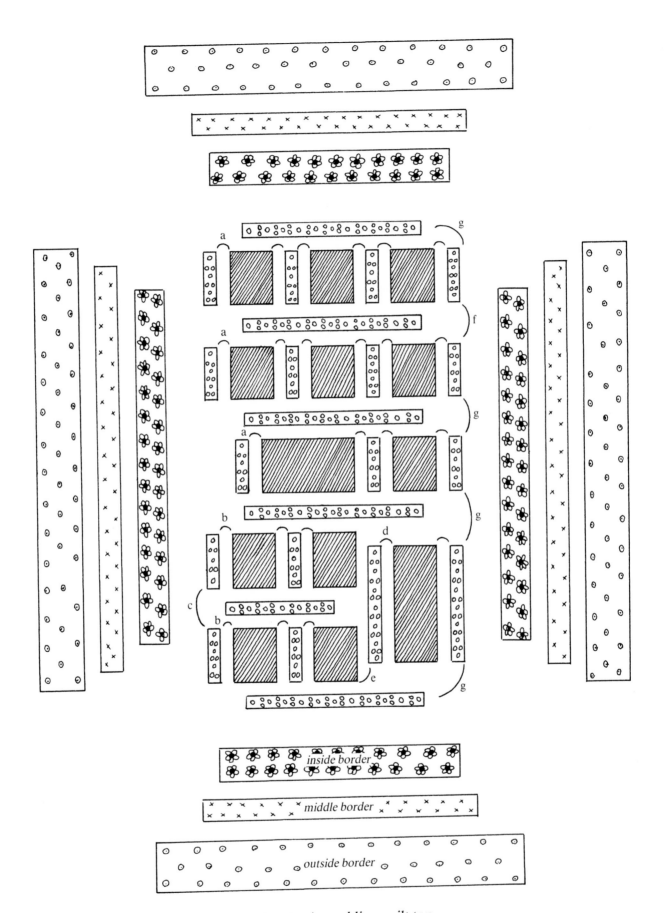

Fig. 4 *Assembling quilt top*

Prepare sashing

12. On wrong side of sashing fabric, mark 2″ strips across fabric, leaving room for ½″ seam allowances. Then measure and cut lengths needed, adding ½″ seam allowances. You will need:

five strips, 2x38″ each
two strips, 2x26″ each
one strip, 2x24″
fifteen strips, 2x12″ each

Assemble center of quilt top

When joining pieces, pin right sides together, carefully matching pencil lines and corner points.

13. Arrange blocks, following photo, page 122, and Fig. 4 as guides.

Work with the three top horizontal rows. Place a 2x12″ sashing strip between blocks and at the end of each row. Pin and stitch blocks and sashing strips together to make three rows (a). *Note:* After each seam is stitched, trim seam allowances on blocks and sashing to ¼″. Continue trimming seams as you assemble center panel.

14. On the fourth and fifth rows, place a 2x12″ sashing strip between the 12″-high blocks and at the left ends. Join these blocks and sashing strips to make two short horizontal rows (b). Place a 2x24″ sashing strip between these rows and stitch the unit together (c).

Stitch a 2x26″ sashing strip to each side of the Gone Fishin' block (d). Then add this unit to complete the last two rows (e).

15. Place a long 2x38″ sashing strip between row units and at top and bottom.

16. Stitch the first and second rows to the sashing strip between them (f). Finish embroidery work by connecting string on kite (Row 1, block 2) to string held by boy (Row 2, block 3). Lightly draw a pencil line across the sashing connecting the lines. Embroider the final line, using black floss and a chain stitch.

17. Stitch remaining sashing strips to rows (g) to complete the center of the quilt. Trim outside seam allowance on sashing to ¼″.

Cut borders

18. For inside border, make a template 6″ wide and about 15″ long. Place template on wrong side of dark blue print and mark along the lengthwise grain, leaving room for ¼″ seam allowances. Mark two strips, 6x72″ each (for sides), and two strips, 6x50″ each (for top and bottom). Cut out, adding ¼″ seam allowances on all edges.

19. For middle border, make a template 4″ wide and about 15″ long. Place template on back of medium green print and mark along the lengthwise grain, leaving room for ¼″ seam allowances. Mark two strips, 4x84″ each (for sides), and two strips, 4x58″ each (for top and bottom). Cut out, adding ¼″ seam allowances on all edges.

Note: If you plan to piece the middle border strips, cut each strip in two sections, adding ¼″ seam allowances for piecing.

20. For outside border, make two templates, each about 15″ long—one 9½″ wide and one 10½″ wide.

On wrong side of medium rust print, mark outside border pieces. Begin by marking two strips, 9½x92″ each (for sides); allow 2″ seam allowance on one long side and ¼″ seam allowances on other three edges (Fig. 5). Also mark one strip 10½x77″ (for top); allow 2″ seam allowances on each end and one long side, and ¼″ seam allowance on other long side. Cut out fabric, adding seam allowances noted.

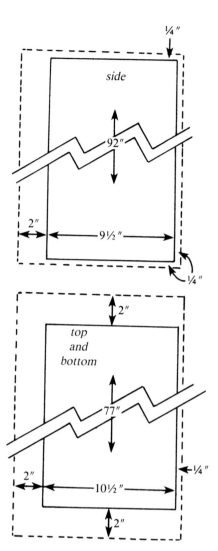

Fig. 5 *Marking outside border pieces*

On next section of fabric, mark one strip 10½x77″ (for bottom); allow 2″ seam allowances on each end and one long side, and ¼″ seam allowance on other long side. Cut out fabric, adding seam allowances noted. (This leaves a wide piece for middle section of backing.)

The 2″ border seam allowances are for turning outside border to overlap the backing; pencil lines mark the fold lines. To transfer fold lines to the right side, hand-baste over pencil lines on all pieces (three lines on top and bottom pieces and one line on each side piece).

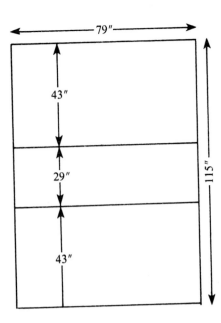

Fig. 6 *Piecing backing (add ½" seam allowances for inside seams)*

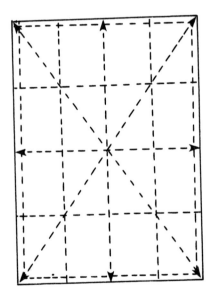

Fig. 7 *Basting quilt layers*

Along the 2" seam allowances, turn each raw edge ½" to the wrong side and press. (Keep this ½" fold open when joining border strip to other border pieces.)

Add borders, piece backing

When joining pieces, pin right sides together, carefully matching pencil lines.

21. Lay border strips in position at top, bottom and sides, with blue print strips next to center of quilt, green print in middle and rust print outside. (Keep basted fold lines on rust strips to the outside.)

22. Pin and stitch border strips to center of quilt, beginning with the blue print. For each color, add the side strips first, then the top and bottom.

23. For backing, cut and piece remaining rust print fabric, following Fig. 6. This allows 1" extra on all outside edges which will be trimmed after quilting.

Stack and quilt

24. Place backing on floor, right side down. Add a layer of batting, piecing it to make correct size; butt strips together and join with loose hand stitches.

Center quilt top over batting and backing, right side up; top will extend beyond other layers. Pin layers together. Baste to hold, sewing from center to each corner and from center to each edge. Add horizontal and vertical lines of basting (Fig. 7). Try to have no open (unbasted) area larger than 6" square.

25. For quilting, use a quilting hoop or frame to keep layers from shifting. Begin at center and work evenly toward outside edges.

Use quilting thread to match or contrast and a small running stitch. Quilt around appliqué shapes, ¼" from seam lines (Fig. 8). Add any other quilting lines you wish.

Fig. 8 *Quilting block*

Quilt inside each block, ¼" from seam lines. Quilt sashing around each block, ¼" from seams, and around center panel, ¼" from border seams.

On each border strip, quilt ¼" from seam lines. On outside border pieces, add an extra quilting line down the middle. (You can use masking tape to mark the lines, and quilt along the tape.)

Finish edges

26. Trim batting and backing to match fold (basted) lines on outside border.

Turn outside edge of border ½" to wrong side (along the pressed line).

To miter each corner, fold border fabric diagonally across corner onto backing (Fig. 9). Fold one edge of border onto backing along fold (basted) line (Fig. 10). Fold adjoining border edge along fold line, forming miter at corner (Fig. 11).

By hand, sew mitered edges together at each corner, and sew straight edges of border to backing.

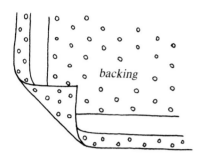

Fig. 9 *Folding corner to begin miter*

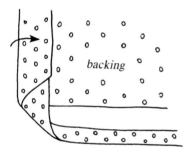

Fig. 10 *Folding first border edge onto backing*

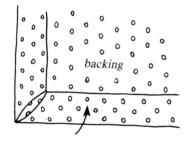

Fig. 11 *Folding adjacent border edge onto backing*

WALL HANGING

(color photo, page 119)

Select one block pattern and the fabrics you wish to use. Frame the block with sashing strips, and finish the outside edges by folding the sashing onto the backing.

1. Follow *Make Blocks* directions for quilt (see Steps 4-11).

2. For sashing frame, make a template 2½" wide and about 10" long. On wrong side of fabric, mark two strips (for sides), each 2½" wide and the same length as the side of the block (12" for most blocks; 26" for Gone Fishin'). On each strip, mark 1½" seam allowance on one long side and ½" seam allowances on the three other edges. Cut out, adding the seam allowances noted.

Place a sashing strip (along the ½" seam allowance) against each side of the block, right sides together. Pin along seam lines and stitch. Trim seam allowances to ¼" and press toward the sashing.

3. Mark two more sashing strips (for top and bottom), each 2½" wide and as long as the width of the block plus the full side strips (18" for most blocks; 30" for Peaceful Moments). On each strip, allow 1½" seam allowance on one long edge, and ½" seam allowance on the other long

edge. Cut out, adding the seam allowances noted.

Stitch one strip to the top and one strip to the bottom of the block. Trim seam allowances to ¼" and press toward the sashing.

4. Mark turning lines. (These are the 1½" seam allowances on the sashing frame.) To transfer these lines to the right side, baste over the pencil lines.

Quilt and finish

5. For backing, mark and cut a piece of fabric the size of the finished wall hanging (15x17" for most blocks; 17x27" for Peaceful Moment; 15x31" for Gone Fishin').

6. Stack layers for quilting. Lay backing fabric flat, right side down. Add batting, cut the same size as the backing. On top, center appliquéd block, right side up. Pin and baste layers together.

7. Quilt block (see Step 25 under quilt directions). You can quilt without a hoop or frame if you wish.

8. To finish edges, turn raw edges of sashing strips ½" to wrong side and press.

Fold sashing strips along fold (basted) lines onto backing and pin. Miter corners and hem sashing to backing (see Step 26 under quilt directions).

9. To make sleeve for hanging, cut a strip of fabric 3" wide and the length of the quilted picture.

Hem the short ends. Turn raw edges ¼" to wrong side and press; make a second turn to the wrong side, press and machine-stitch.

On the long sides, turn raw edges ½" to wrong side and press.

10. Position sleeve on back, just below top edge of quilted picture. Sew long edges to back by hand.

11. Slip a rod through sleeve to hang quilted picture on wall.

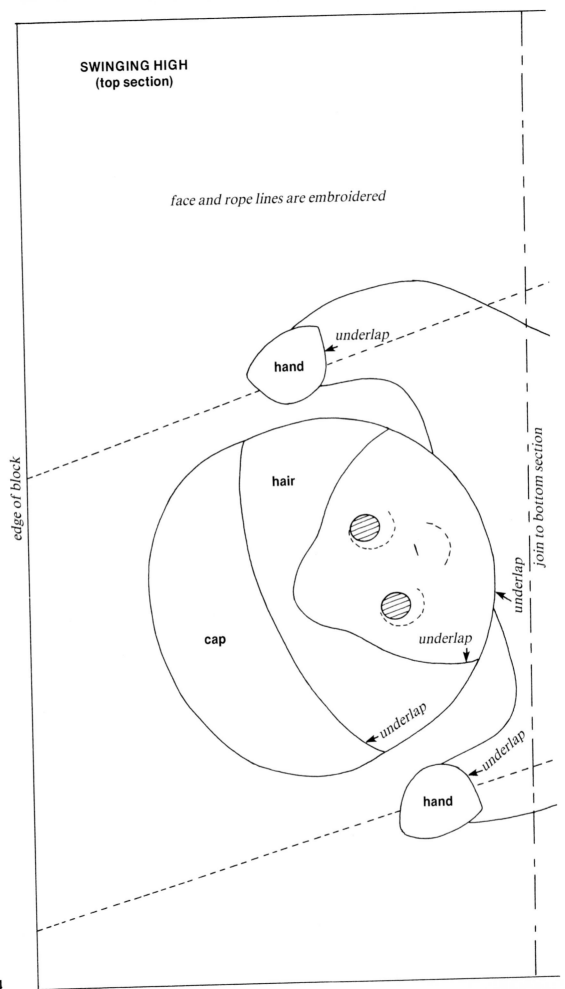

SWINGING HIGH
(top section)

face and rope lines are embroidered

underlap

edge of block

join to bottom section

hand

hair

underlap

cap

underlap

underlap

underlap

hand

underlap

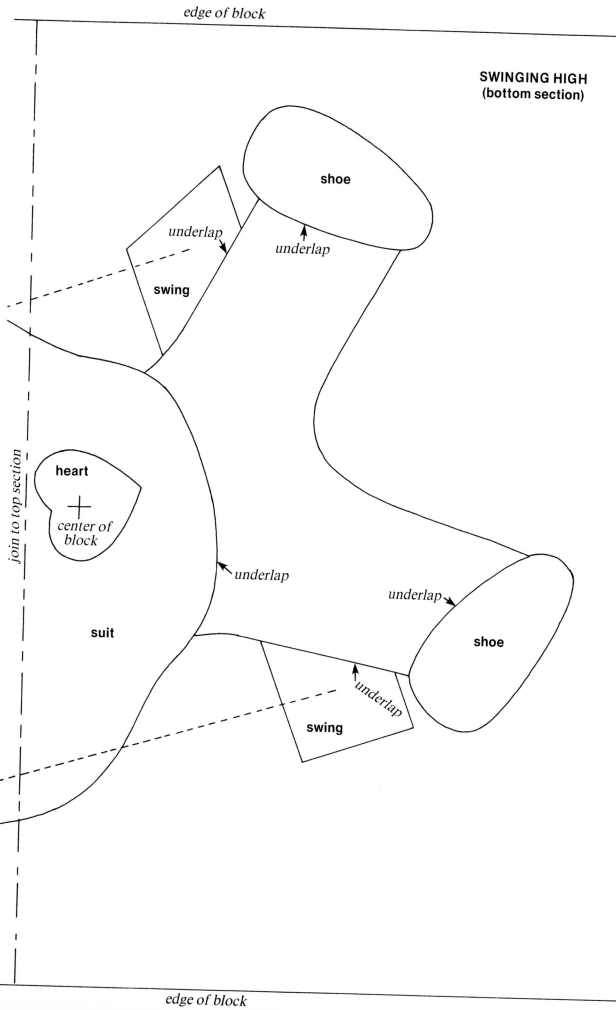

edge of block

SWINGING HIGH
(bottom section)

shoe

underlap

swing

underlap

underlap

heart

center of block

underlap

suit

underlap

shoe

underlap

swing

join to top section

edge of block

edge of block

edge of block

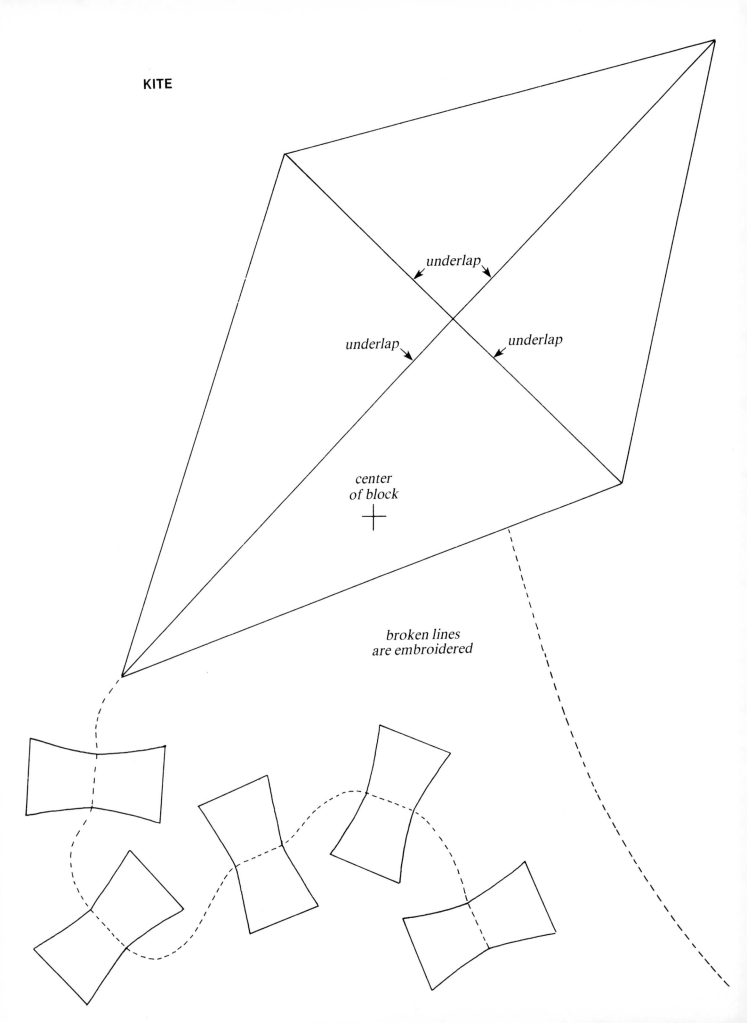

KITE

underlap

underlap *underlap*

*center
of block*

*broken lines
are embroidered*

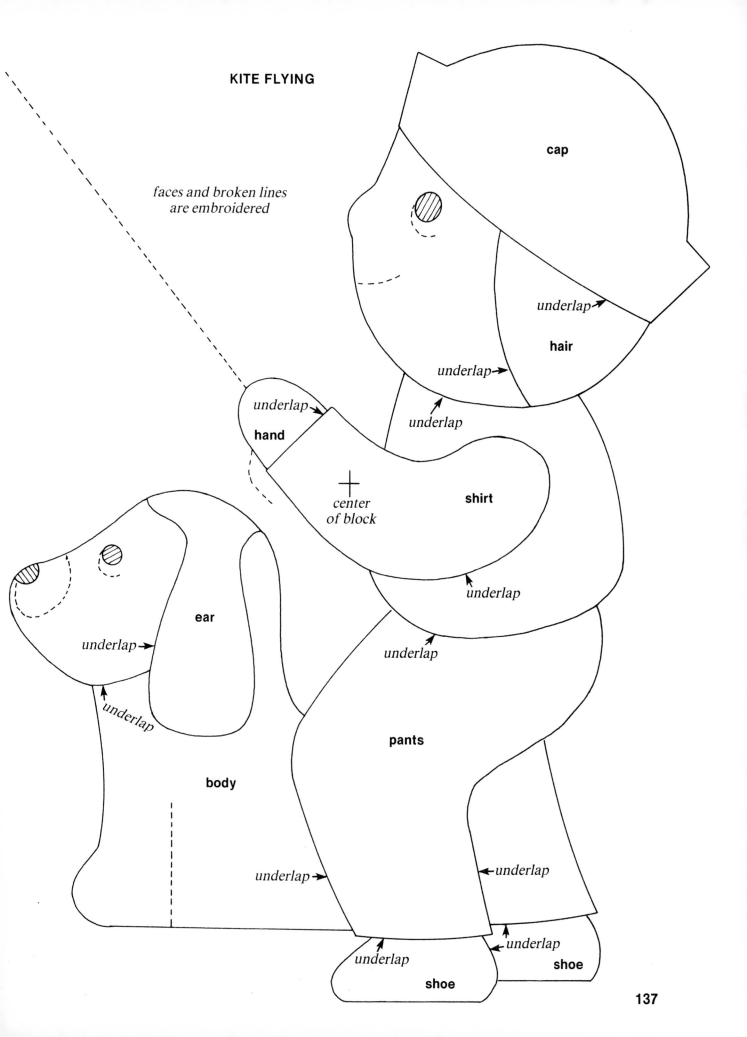

KITE FLYING

faces and broken lines are embroidered

cap

underlap

hair

underlap

underlap

underlap

hand

center of block

shirt

underlap

ear

underlap

underlap

underlap

pants

body

underlap

underlap

underlap

underlap

shoe

shoe

137

TEDDY BEAR

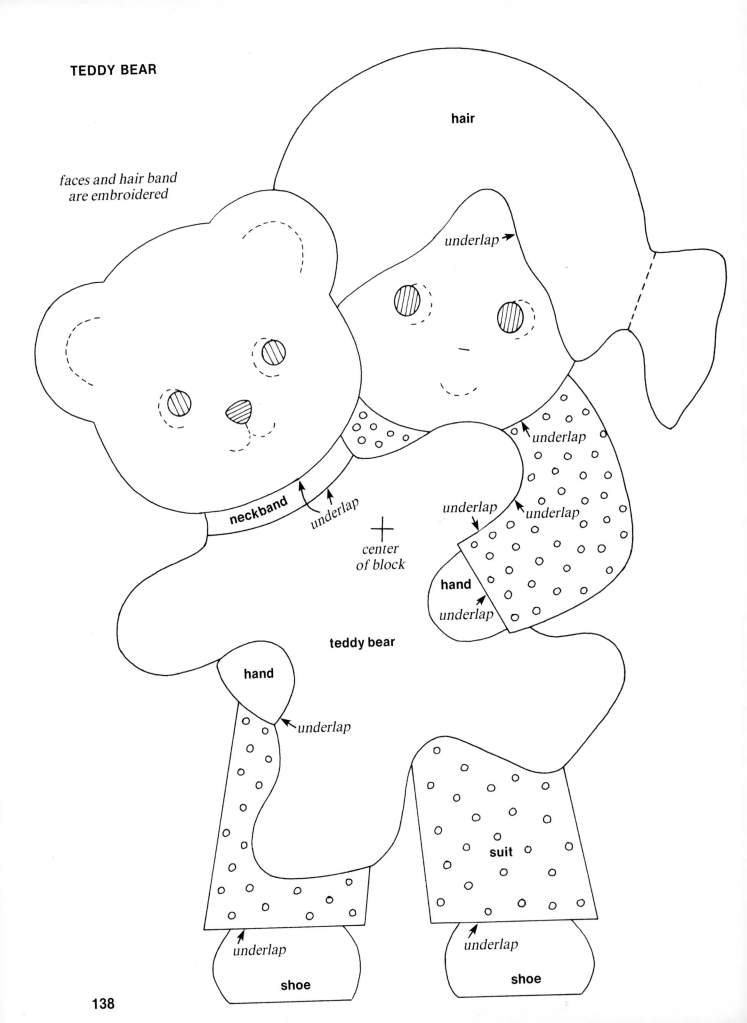

faces and hair band are embroidered

hair

underlap

underlap

underlap

underlap

neckband

underlap

+

center of block

hand

underlap

hand

teddy bear

underlap

underlap

suit

underlap

underlap

shoe

shoe

138

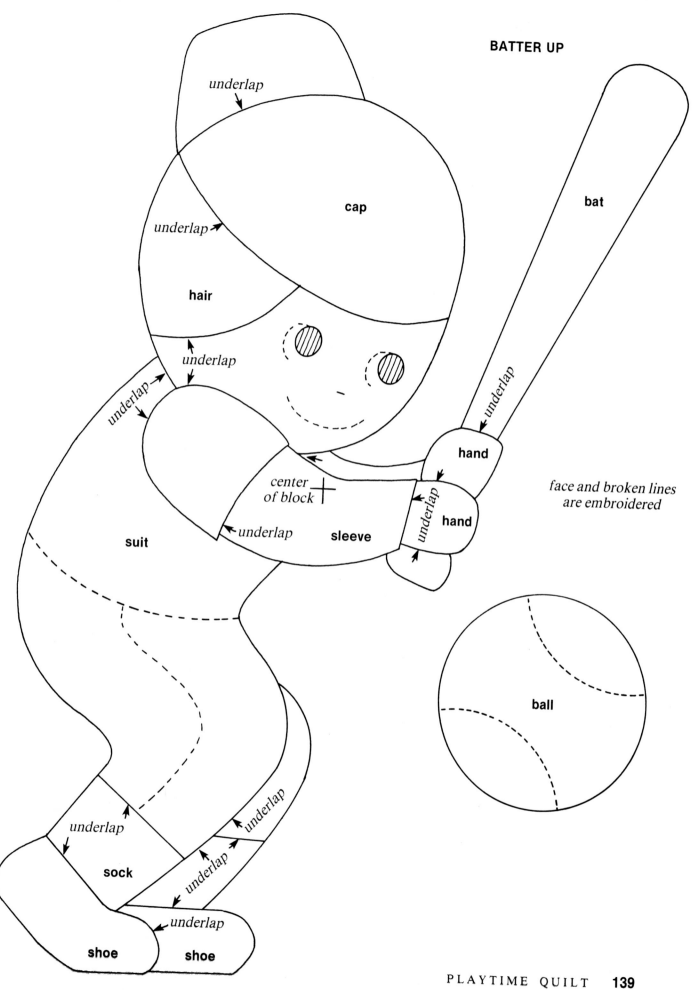

BATTER UP

underlap

cap

bat

underlap

hair

underlap

underlap

underlap

underlap

hand

center
of block

underlap

hand

suit

underlap

sleeve

*face and broken lines
are embroidered*

ball

underlap

underlap

sock

underlap

underlap

shoe

shoe

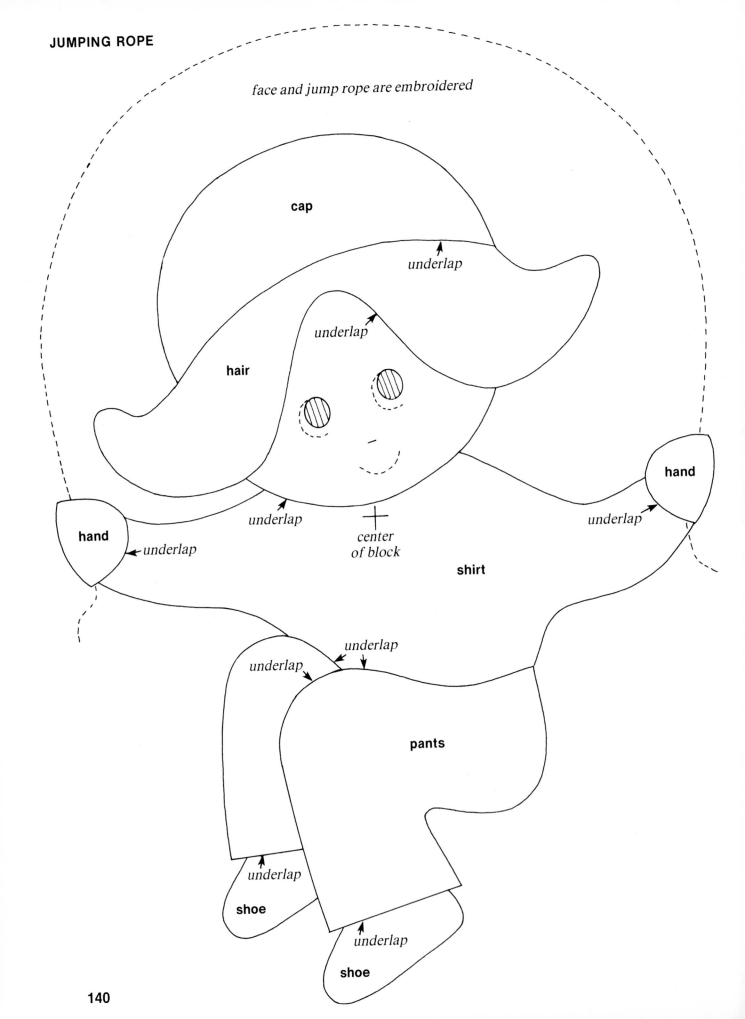

face and jump rope are embroidered

cap

underlap

underlap

hair

underlap

center
of block

hand

underlap

hand

underlap

shirt

underlap

underlap

pants

underlap

shoe

underlap

shoe

PEACEFUL MOMENT
(left section)

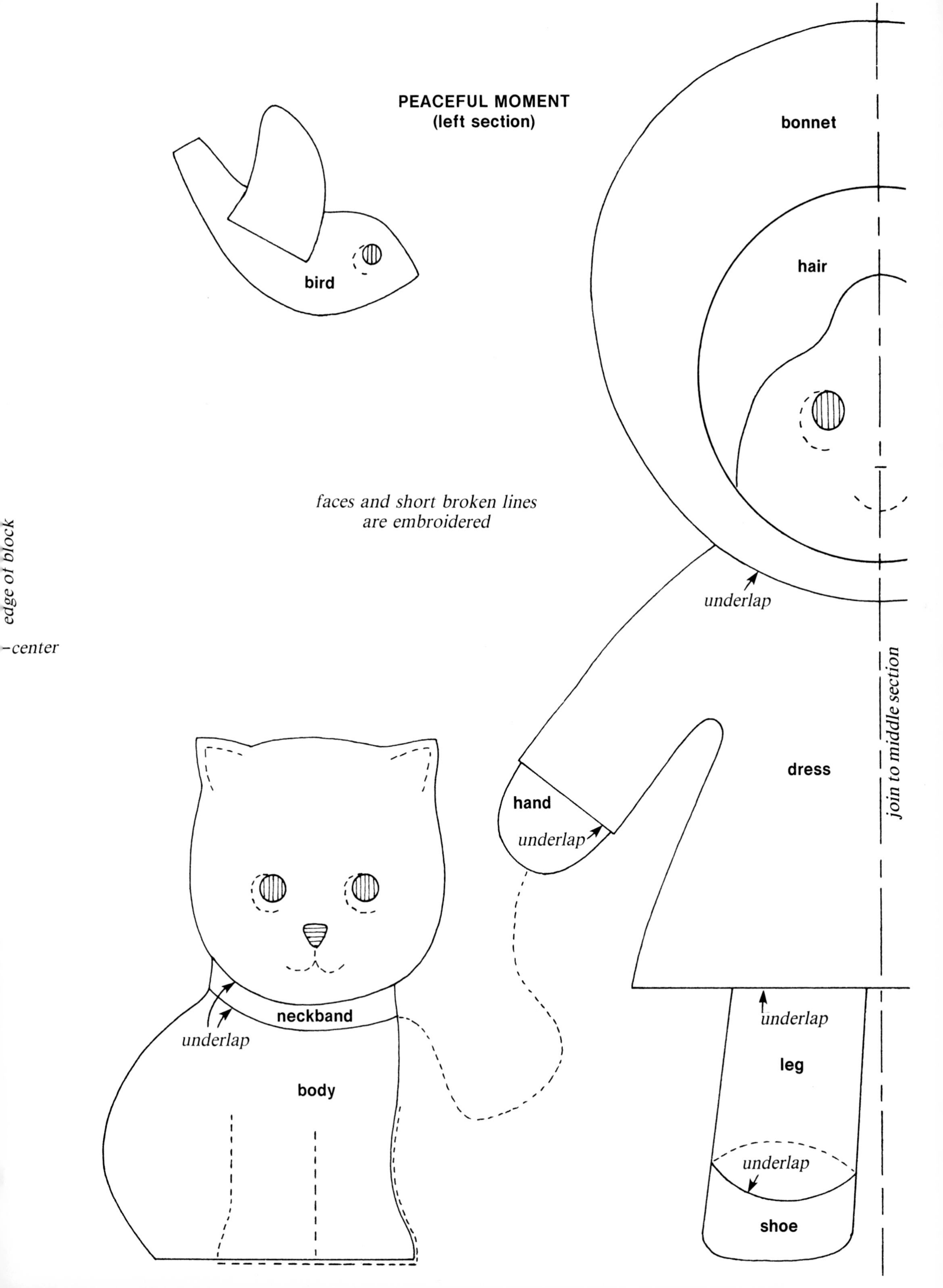

bird

bonnet

hair

*faces and short broken lines
are embroidered*

edge of block

—center

underlap

join to middle section

dress

hand

underlap

neckband

underlap

body

underlap

leg

underlap

shoe

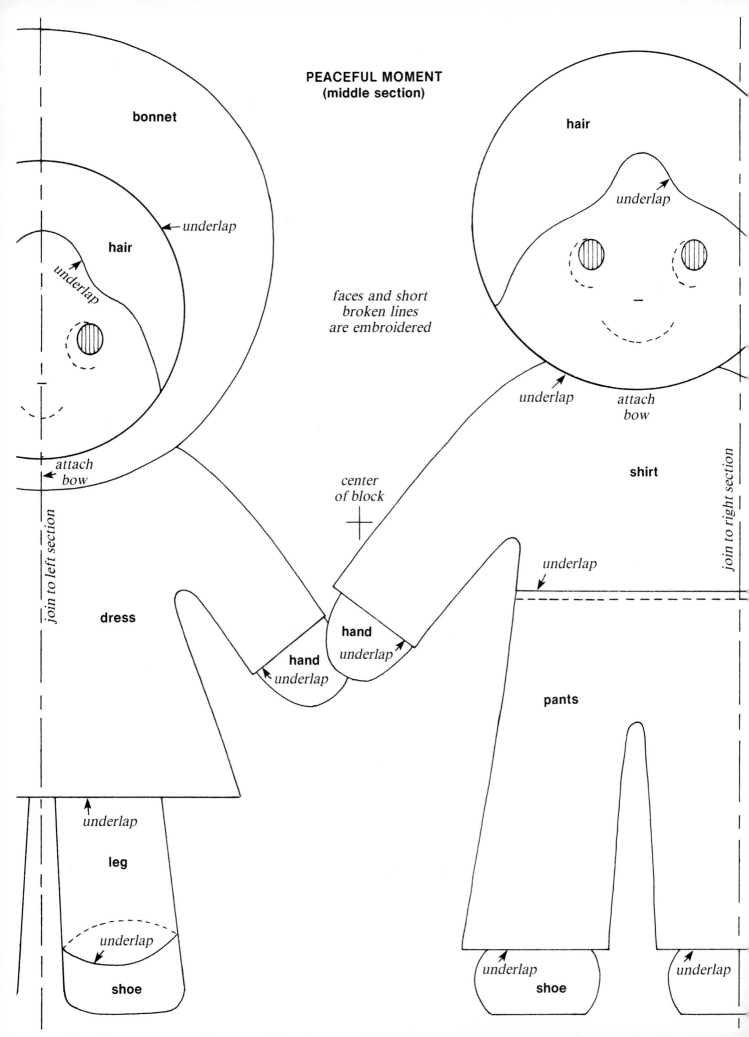

PEACEFUL MOMENT
(middle section)

bonnet

hair

underlap

underlap

hair

underlap

faces and short
broken lines
are embroidered

attach
bow

underlap

attach
bow

shirt

center
of block

join to left section

join to right section

dress

underlap

hand

hand

underlap

underlap

pants

underlap

leg

underlap

underlap

shoe

underlap

shoe

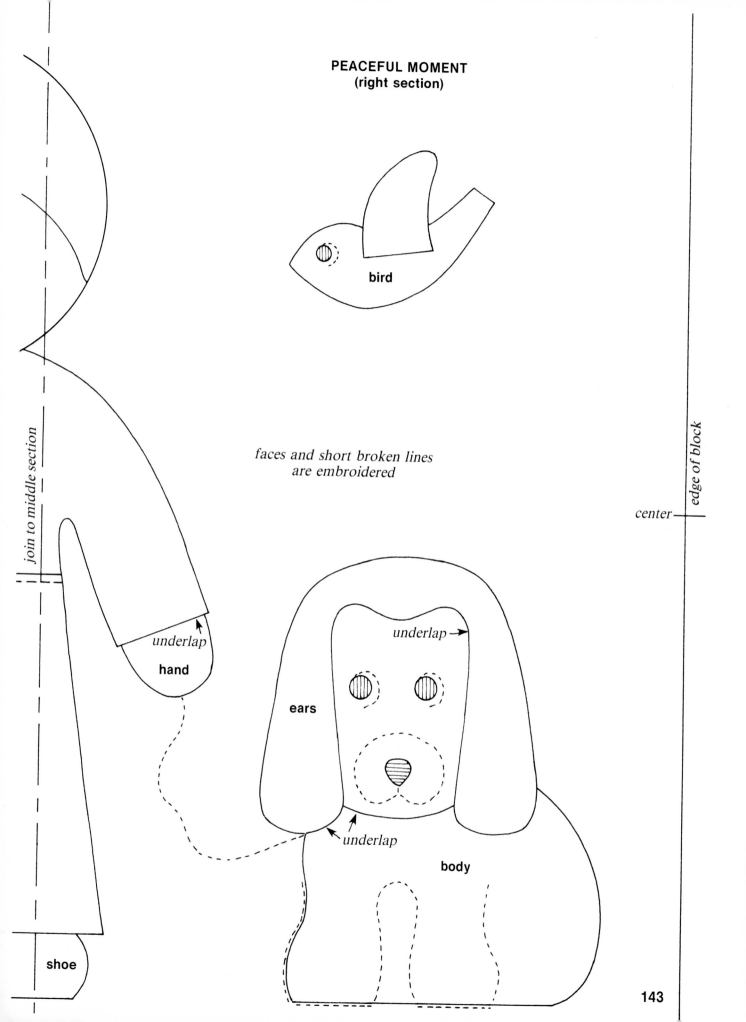

PEACEFUL MOMENT
(right section)

bird

join to middle section

*faces and short broken lines
are embroidered*

edge of block

center

underlap

hand

underlap

ears

underlap

body

shoe

143

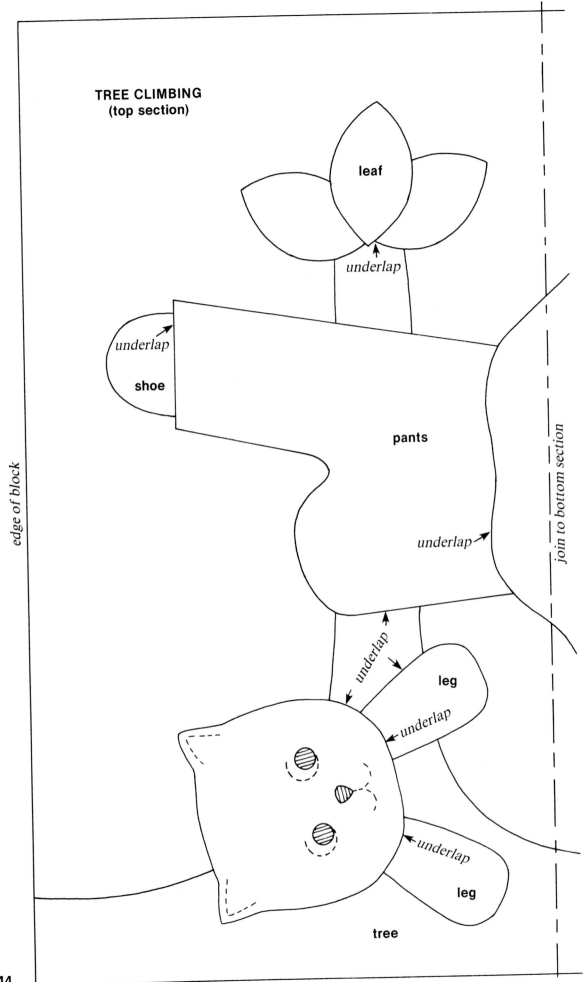

TREE CLIMBING
(top section)

leaf

underlap

edge of block

underlap

shoe

pants

underlap

join to bottom section

underlap

leg

underlap

underlap

leg

tree

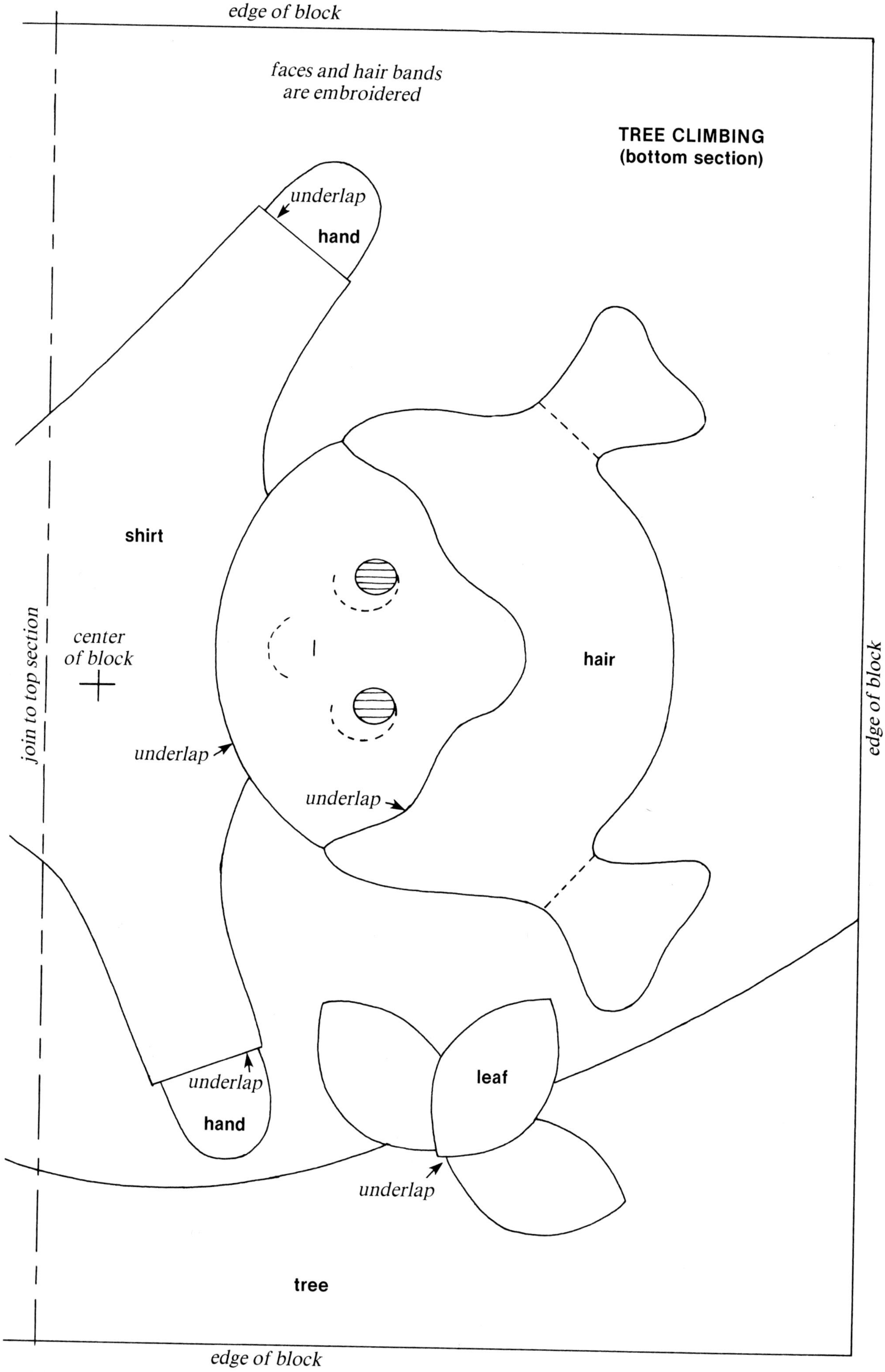

edge of block

faces and hair bands
are embroidered

**TREE CLIMBING
(bottom section)**

underlap

hand

shirt

join to top section

*center
of block*

hair

underlap

underlap

edge of block

underlap

hand

leaf

underlap

tree

edge of block

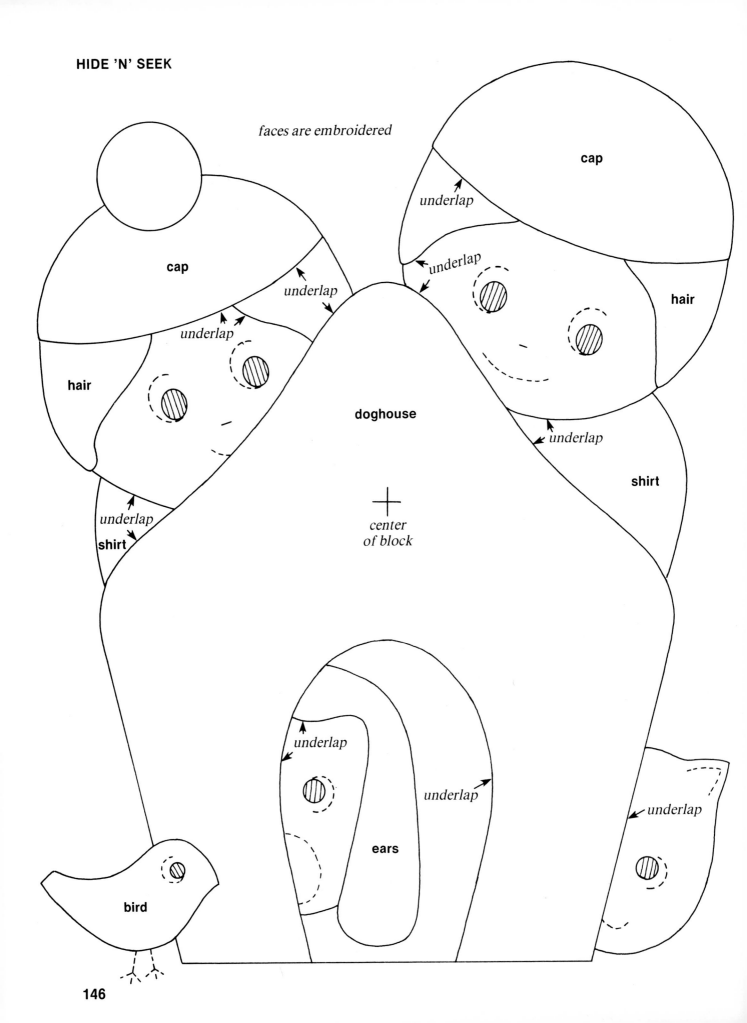

HIDE 'N' SEEK

faces are embroidered

cap

cap

underlap

underlap

underlap

hair

underlap

hair

doghouse

underlap

shirt

+

center
of block

shirt

underlap

underlap

underlap

ears

bird

146

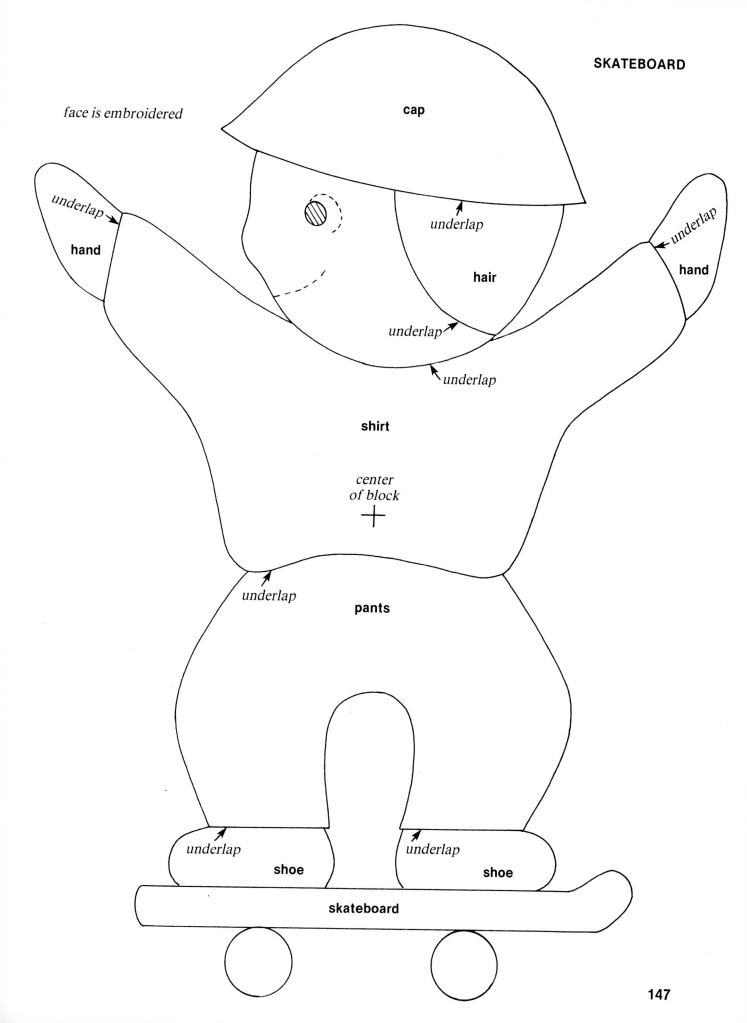

SKATEBOARD

face is embroidered

cap

underlap

hand

underlap

hair

underlap

underlap

hand

underlap

shirt

center
of block

underlap

pants

underlap

shoe

underlap

shoe

skateboard

147

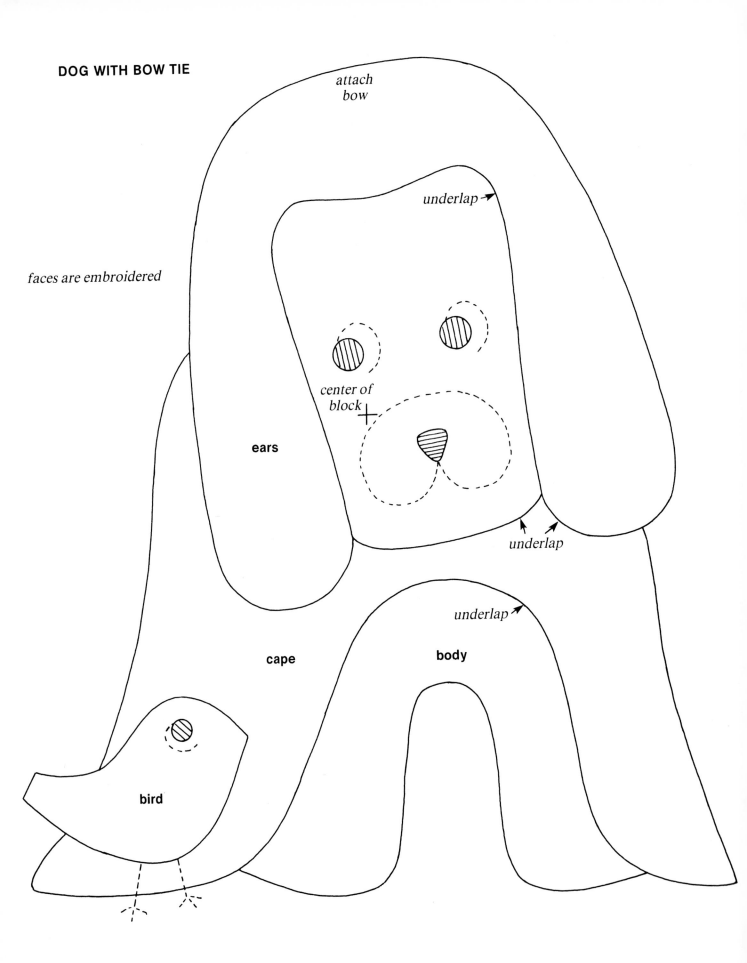

DOG WITH BOW TIE

attach bow

underlap →

faces are embroidered

center of block +

ears

underlap ↑ ↑

cape   **body**

underlap →

bird

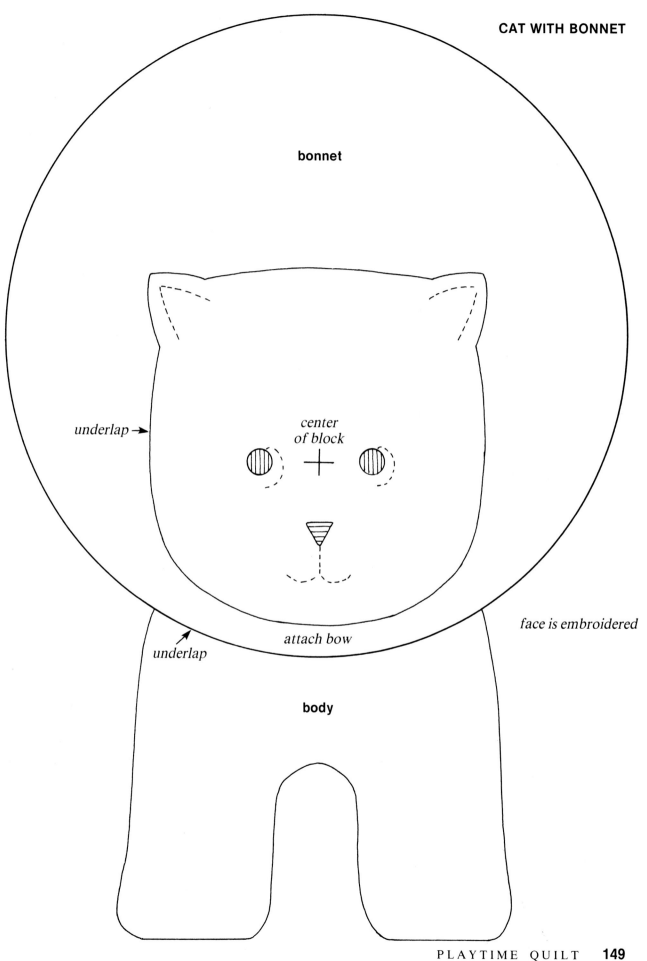

bonnet

underlap →

center
of block

underlap

attach bow

face is embroidered

body

top edge of block
center

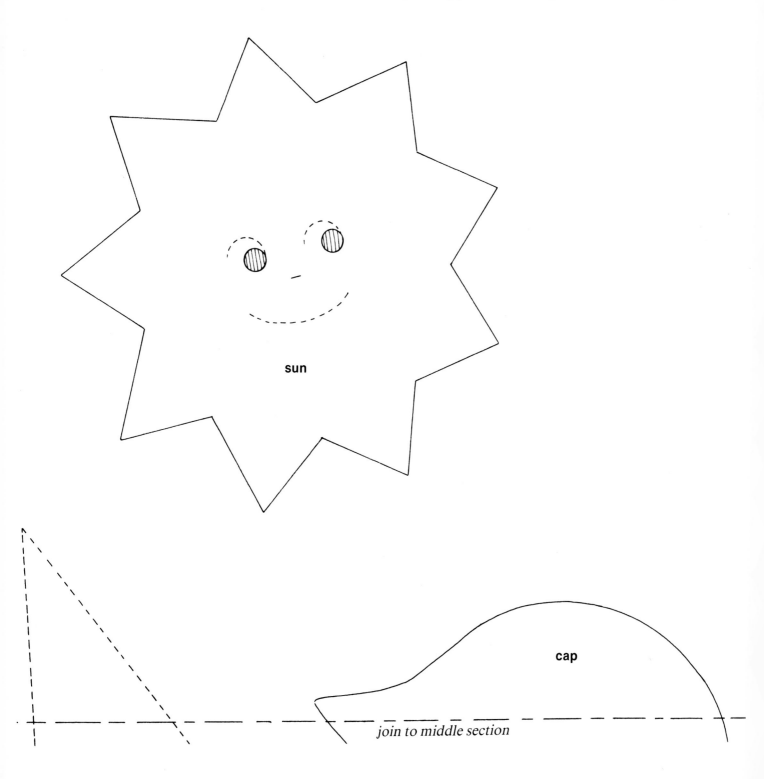

GONE FISHIN'
(top section)

faces, fishing pole and fishing line are embroidered

sun

cap

join to middle section

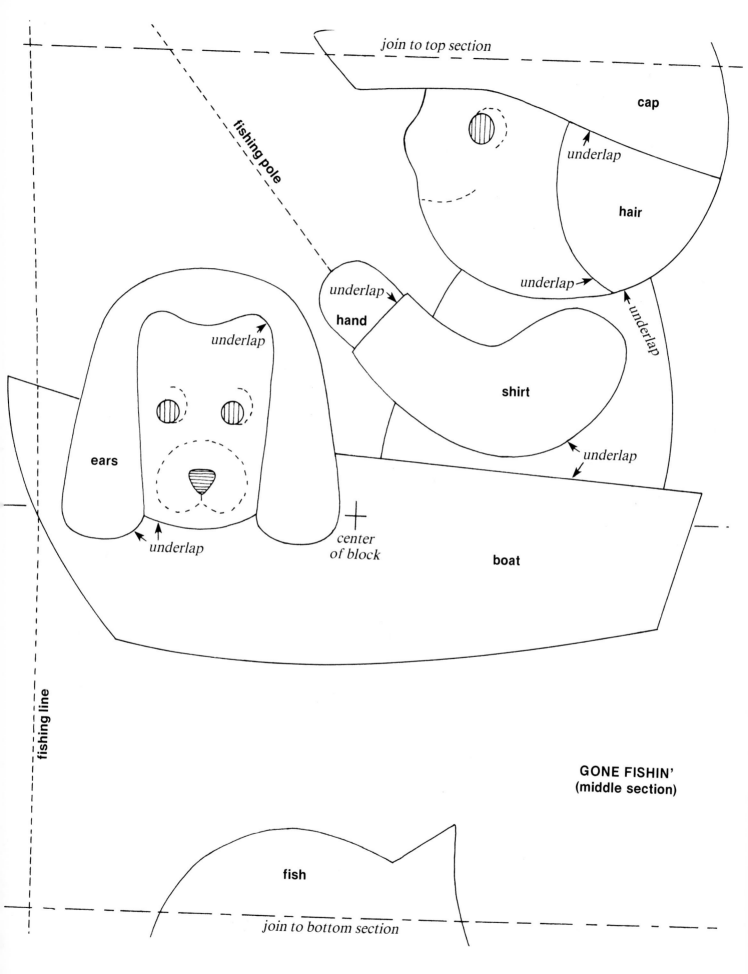

join to top section

cap

underlap

fishing pole

hair

underlap

underlap

underlap

hand

shirt

underlap

ears

underlap

center
of block

boat

fishing line

GONE FISHIN'
(middle section)

fish

join to bottom section

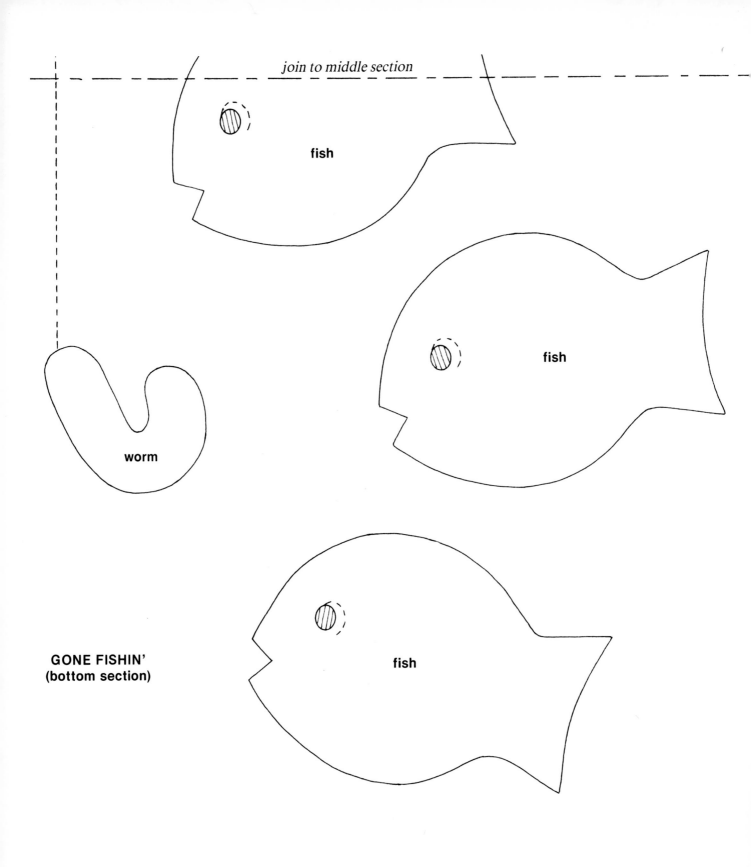

join to middle section

fish

worm

fish

GONE FISHIN'
(bottom section)

fish

center
bottom edge block

Index